Sylvia
Plath

COMPREHENSIVE RESEARCH
AND STUDY GUIDE

Sylvia Plath

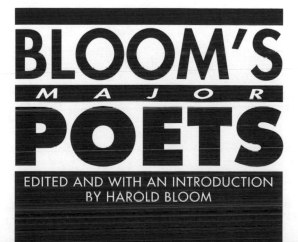

EDITED AND WITH AN INTRODUCTION
BY HAROLD BLOOM

© 2001 by Chelsea House Publishers,
a subsidiary of Haights Cross Communications.

Introduction © 2001 by Harold Bloom.

Printed and bound in the United States of America.

9 8 7 6 5 4 3 2

Library of Congress Cataloging-in-Publication Data
Sylvia Plath / edited and with an introduction by Harold Bloom.
        p. cm. — (Bloom's major poets)
    Includes bibliographical references and index.
    ISBN 0-7910-5935-9 (alk. paper)
    1. Plath, Sylvia—Criticism and interpretation—Handbooks,
manuals, etc. 2. Plath, Sylvia—Examinations—Study guides.
    I. Bloom, Harold. II. Series.
    PS3566.L27 Z914 2000
    811'.54—dc21   00-055590
                                                   CIP

Chelsea House Publishers
1974 Sproul Road, Suite 400
Broomall, PA 19008-0914

www.chelseahouse.com

Contributing Editor: Pamela Loos

Produced by: Robert Gerson Publisher's Services, Santa Barbara, CA

Contents

User's Guide   7

Editor's Note   8

Introduction   9

Biography of Sylvia Plath   11

Thematic Analysis of "The Colossus"   15
Critical Views on "The Colossus"   18
  J. D. McClatchy on Plath's Growth   18
  Ted Hughes on Plath's Poetic Styles   20
  Lynda K. Bundtzen on the Daughter's Opposing Perspectives   22
  Robyn Marsack on the Poem's Views on Our Unending Searches   24
  Elisabeth Bronfen on the Colossal Womb-Tomb   26

Thematic Analysis of "The Arrival of the Bee Box"   29
Critical Views on "The Arrival of the Bee Box"   32
  Rose Kamel on the Bees' Counter-aggression as Political Commentary   32
  Mary Lynn Broe on the Power Switch   34
  Susan R. Van Dyne on the Maternal and Paternal Tugs of War   36
  Malin Walther Pereira on Plath's Racism   38

Thematic Analysis of "Daddy"   41
Critical Views on "Daddy"   45
  A. Alvarez on Plath's Concern with Loss of Identity   45
  Joyce Carol Oates on Plath's Isolation   47
  Brian Murdoch on the Historical Use of Genocide Imagery   49
  Elizabeth Hardwick on Plath's Revolutionary Daring   51
  Jacqueline Rose on the Missing Communication   52
  Jahan Ramazani on Plath's Revamping of the Elegy   54
  Elisabeth Bronfen on the Narrator's Confrontation with
    Her Family History   55

Thematic Analysis of "Ariel"   58
Critical Views on "Ariel"   61
  William V. Davis on the Allusion to Jerusalem   61
  Anthony Libby on Plath's Internalization of the Apocalypse   63
  D. F. McKay on Plath's Technique for Describing Divine Energy   65
  Linda Wagner on Plath's References to Shakespeare's Ariel   68
  Lynda K. Bundtzen on "Ariel" as Plath at Her Most Triumphant   70
  Susan R. Van Dyne on the Incarnations of the Speaker in "Ariel" 71

Thematic Analysis of "Lady Lazarus"   74
Critical Views on "Lady Lazarus"   78
  Robert Bagg on Plath's Refusal to Accept the Self's Limitations   78
  Irving Howe on Plath's Weakness   79
  Jon Rosenblatt on the Sounds of the Poem   81
  Fred Moramarco on the Literal Destructiveness of Plath's Later Style 83
  Lynda K. Bundtzen on the Poem's Comment on Female Authorship   86
  Alicia Suskin Ostriker on Plath's Solutions for Detachment   87

Works by Sylvia Plath   90
Works About Sylvia Plath   91
Index of Themes and Ideas   95

User's Guide

This volume is designed to present biographical, critical, and bibliographical information on the author's best-known or most important poems. Following Harold Bloom's editor's note and introduction is a detailed biography of the author, discussing major life events and important literary accomplishments. A thematic and structural analysis of each poem follows, tracing significant themes, patterns, and motifs in the work.

A selection of critical extracts, derived from previously published material from leading critics, analyzes aspects of each poem. The extracts consist of statements from the author, if available, early reviews of the work, and later evaluations up to the present. A bibliography of the author's writings (including a complete list of all books written, cowritten, edited, and translated), a list of additional books and articles on the author and the work, and an index of themes and ideas in the author's writings conclude the volume.

~

Harold Bloom is Sterling Professor of the Humanities at Yale University and Henry W. and Albert A. Berg Professor of English at the New York University Graduate School. He is the author of over 20 books, including *Shelley's Mythmaking* (1959), *The Visionary Company* (1961), *Blake's Apocalypse* (1963), *Yeats* (1970), *A Map of Misreading* (1975), *Kabbalah and Criticism* (1975), *Agon: Toward a Theory of Revisionism* (1982), *The American Religion* (1992), *The Western Canon* (1994), and *Omens of Millennium: The Gnosis of Angels, Dreams, and Resurrection* (1996). *The Anxiety of Influence* (1973) sets forth Professor Bloom's provocative theory of the literary relationships between the great writers and their predecessors. His most recent books include *Shakespeare: The Invention of the Human*, a 1998 National Book Award finalist, and *How to Read and Why*, which was published in 2000.

Professor Bloom earned his Ph.D. from Yale University in 1955 and has served on the Yale faculty since then. He is a 1985 MacArthur Foundation Award recipient, served as the Charles Eliot Norton Professor of Poetry at Harvard University in 1987–88, and has received honorary degrees from the universities of Rome and Bologna. In 1999, Professor Bloom received the prestigious American Academy of Arts and Letters Gold Medal for Criticism.

Currently, Harold Bloom is the editor of numerous Chelsea House volumes of literary criticism, including the series BLOOM'S NOTES, BLOOM'S MAJOR DRAMATISTS, BLOOM'S MAJOR NOVELISTS, MAJOR LITERARY CHARACTERS, MODERN CRITICAL VIEWS, MODERN CRITICAL INTERPRETATIONS, and WOMEN WRITERS OF ENGLISH AND THEIR WORKS.

Editor's Note

My Introduction intimates some continued reservations as to Plath's poetic eminence, while acknowledging that she has become an instance of Popular Poetry.

The Critical Views extracted are very varied, ranging from the passionate advocacy of Susan R. Van Dyne and Jacqueline Rose through the more measured esteem of J. D. McClatchy on to the strictures of Robert Bagg and Irving Howe.

It seems valid to observe, in all mildness, that the question of Plath's permanence remains unsettled.

Introduction

HAROLD BLOOM

Sylvia Plath, who killed herself early in 1963 at age thirty, is widely regarded as a major poet, particularly in her posthumously published volume *Ariel* (1965). It is unwise to quarrel with Plath's partisans, because one can never be sure precisely what the disagreement concerns. I have just reread *Ariel*, and confess myself moved by the quality of pathos the book evokes. And yet I remain unpersuaded that *Ariel* is a permanent work; that is, poetry of authentic eminence. American poetry in the twentieth century is immensely rich in women of genius: Gertrude Stein, Hilda Doolittle, Marianne Moore, Louise Bogan, Léonie Adams, Laura Riding, Elizabeth Bishop, May Swenson, Amy Clampitt, and several living poets. If one adds the great Canadian poet Anne Carson—who is the peer of any poet now alive—one can say that an extraordinary standard has been set. By that measure, Plath is scarcely to be described as more than sincere.

And yet Plath clearly answers a need, neither aesthetic nor cognitive, but profoundly affective. In that sense, she remains a representative writer and the phenomenon of her popularity is worthy of critical meditation. Perhaps she should be consigned to the category of popular poetry, with the very different (and wonderfully good-natured) Maya Angelou. Since Plath's masters included Stevens, Auden, and Roethke, while Angelou relies upon black folk poetry, my comparison must seem initially a little strange. But surely what matters about Plath, as about Angelou, is the audience. These are poems for people who don't read poems, though in Plath's case one must add feminist ideologues, who regard her as an exemplary martyr to patriarchal nastiness.

This volume contains fierce partisans of Plath, among whom the formidable Jacqueline Rose is the most passionate. There are also a few dissenters, who find Plath to be racist or a touch too anxious to appropriate the Holocaust for her personal purposes. I pass on such matters; for me the issue is elsewhere, and is always aesthetic:

> Herr God, Herr Lucifer
> Beware
> Beware

Out of the ash
I rise with my red hair
And I eat men like air.

I cite the High Modernist critic Hugh Kenner, a close reader of Pound, Eliot, and Joyce:

> The death poems—say a third of *Ariel*—are bad for anyone's soul. They give a look of literary respectability to voyeurist passions: no gain for poetry, nor for her.

That seems (to me) very difficult to refute, unless you are a glutton for the confessional mode. Popular poetry is an ally of true confessions, an alliance that never will end. ✦

Biography of
Sylvia Plath

The daughter of scholarly parents, Sylvia Plath published her first poem at the age of eight in the *Boston Sunday Herald*. She continued to write, and while a professional writer for only the last seven years of her brief life, she created a plethora of work. In that short seven-year span she finished more than two hundred and fifty poems, several commissioned nonfiction works for magazines and the BBC, possibly as many as seventy short stories, a verse play, a children's book, a novel, and at least one draft of a second novel. In between, she penned an extensive journal and an abundance of letters that were written mostly to her mother.

Aurelia Schober, Plath's mother, was an avid reader who taught English and German at a high school. A German whose parents were from Austria, she met her husband, Otto Plath, at Boston University, where she was a student in one of his classes. Otto had emigrated to New York City from Germany as an adolescent. The two were married in January 1932 and continued to live in Boston.

Sylvia was born on October 27, 1932; her brother Warren was born two-and-a-half years later. The family moved to Winthrop, Massachusetts, when Sylvia was four to be closer to the sea and to Aurelia's parents. Otto Plath suffered from what appeared to be lung cancer; in fact he had treatable diabetes. By the time he received the proper medical attention, he was forced to have a leg amputated as a result of what had started as a gangrenous toe. He never returned home from the hospital after the operation, however, but died from an embolism. It was 1940, both children were still young, and Aurelia's parents moved in with the now-smaller family to provide additional support. Shortly thereafter, when Aurelia was offered a teaching post at a university, the extended family moved inland to Wellesley, Massachusetts.

Sylvia entered Smith College in 1950, receiving three scholarships in her first year. From Smith, Plath wrote home: "I could just cry with happiness. . . . The world is splitting open at my feet like a ripe, juicy watermelon." At the same time, however, her letters reported episodes of severe depression.

In June of 1953 Plath fell into a great depression when she learned she had not been accepted in Frank O'Connor's summer school writing course at Harvard. Bereft, she left her mother a note saying she was going off on a long walk and would return the following day. Then she carefully hid herself in their basement, where she took an overdose of sleeping pills. Three days later Plath was heard moaning, found semiconscious, revived, and hospitalized.

Plath returned to Smith in the spring of 1954 and was one of only four students to graduate that June with the highest possible grade-point average. Winning a Fulbright scholarship to Newham College in Cambridge, England, she set off and immediately built again a very active and very social life. By June of 1956 she had married Ted Hughes, then a relatively unknown poet. She described Hughes as "the only man in the world who is my match."

Upon graduating from Cambridge, Plath and her husband moved back to the States, where Plath took up teaching at Smith. Rather exhausted after the first year there and determined to do more writing, Plath and Hughes moved to Boston. The couple returned to England when they found out Sylvia was pregnant, and she gave birth to their daughter, Freida Rebecca, in April 1960. Just prior to the birth, Plath signed a contract for publication in England of her first book of poetry, *The Colossus and Other Poems*. In 1961 Plath suffered from a miscarriage and from having her appendix removed in emergency surgery. But shortly thereafter, Alfred Knopf bought the rights to produce *The Colossus* in the United States, and Plath quickly received favorable attention and a sizable writing grant from an American foundation. She began working intently on *The Bell Jar*, a novel that contains much autobiographical detail about her near-suicide at age twenty.

By late summer, the couple had moved to the countryside, into a manor house in Devon. While Plath had felt exhilarated after the birth of her first child, she felt strained after giving birth to a son, Nicholas, in January 1962. In May of that year, the Hughes's friends David and Assia Wevill visited them. Plath later learned of an attraction between her husband and Assia. Angered, she burned her manuscript for a second novel that contained many elements about her romance and marriage to Hughes.

May 1962 had also been the month *The Colossus* was released for publication in the United States. In an effort to expend her energy positively, Plath wrote essays, book reviews, and finished her radio play, *Three Women*. She had jubilantly been working to build her husband's writing career; now she honed in on her own.

By August, the couple planned to divorce. Only a few days after making this decision, Plath drove her car off the road, yet was unharmed. By October, Hughes had moved out and Plath rented an apartment in London, where she was most pleased to know one of her favorite poets, William Butler Yeats, had lived. It was here that she wrote feverishly each morning, completing at least one poem a day that month. Few needed much revising, and all embraced a revolutionary new voice. "I am writing the best poems of my life; they will make my name," Plath wrote to her mother, and critics would concur years later when they read the work. "Terrific stuff, as if domesticity had choked me," Plath wrote home. At the same time, she was working on her third novel, *Double Exposure*.

In January of 1963 *The Bell Jar* was published in London under the pseudonym Victoria Lucas. While many reviewers wrote of it favorably, Plath was disappointed that they seemed oblivious to the primary focus on the main character's recovery and rebirth. The poems she sent to publications at this time were slow to be received, also adding to her frustration. Disillusioned from her crumbled marriage, burdened financially, struggling to care for two young children, and affected by the medication she was taking, Plath took many sleeping pills and allowed herself to be consumed by the fumes from the gas oven. She had left a note asking that her doctor be called, and indicating his name and number. As a result, many people assume that she was expecting to be found and revived again, as she had been at 20, especially because the children's nurse was to be at the house early in the morning. However, she was pronounced dead on arrival at the hospital that morning of April 11, 1963.

Ted Hughes, still legally Plath's husband, then took control of her work, getting *Ariel* published in 1965. While Plath had carefully chosen the poetry to include in this book, ending it with her bee poems and their focus on rebirth, Hughes made his own decisions about what to include and in what order, ending the book with imagery of the inevitability of death. In 1971 Hughes published *Crossing the Water*, which contains Plath's poetry that was written after *The Colossus* and up to July 1962. That same year, *Winter Trees* was released; it contained eighteen of Plath's poems as well as her radio play *Three Women*. Plath's poem for children, *The Bed Book*, was published in 1976, and a collection of her prose was published in 1977. Entitled *Johnny Panic and the Bible of Dreams: Short Stories, Prose, and Diary Excerpts*, the title story contains some reflections on Plath's time working at Massachusetts General Hospital.

Aurelia Plath compiled and edited some of her daughter's letters; these were then published in 1975 as *Letters Home: Correspondence 1950–1963*. It took until 1981 for a comprehensive collection of Sylvia Plath's work to appear, *The Collected Poems*, which became one of the few works that has been awarded a Pulitzer Prize posthumously. Shortly after, in 1982, *The Journals of Sylvia Plath* was published. *The It-Doesn't-Matter Suit*, a children's book, was published in 1996. Plath's unabridged journals will be published shortly. They had been sealed from the public by Ted Hughes until a month before he died in 1998. ❁

Thematic Analysis of
"The Colossus"

The Colossus at Rhodes, Greece, was one of the wonders of the ancient world. The term "colossus" also was used generally to refer to statues of great size. The statue at Rhodes was of the Greek sun god. It is estimated to have been 100 to 115 feet high and was destroyed in an earthquake in 224 B.C. Plath's choice of "The Colossus" as the title for her poem and her first collection of poetry, then, conjures images of monumental stone, violent natural destruction, powerful gods, and history. The poem's narrator speaks to her broken colossus throughout the piece. Yet it is not until we are halfway through the poem that the narrator addresses the colossus with "O father," sounding partially like a chiding daughter and partially like a suppliant beginning a prayer to her god. The word "father" should be capitalized here but it is not, even though all other proper nouns in the poem are; both fathers are diminished as a result.

From the poem's first line, we learn that the narrator believes she can never completely repair the monument. He cannot be restructured into the father he was nor the father she always wanted him to be. We also quickly learn by the poem's third line that the narrator's glorified, god-like image of the figure is inappropriate. For this is a statue that makes "bawdy" sounds of base animals like pigs and mules.

Into the second stanza the disparate views of who this colossus is persist. The narrator comments that she believes he might construe himself an oracle. Just as she is helpless to put him back together, so she has been helpless in clearing his throat to enable him to speak and explain. She has been at it for thirty years, we hear. "I am none the wiser," she states, simple words that are open to multiple interpretations. She could be none the wiser because she still doesn't understand who he is, because he was taken from her too early to impart his wisdom to her, and/or because she still cannot discern how to repair him or her image of him.

By the third stanza, the narrator's difficulty seems worse. The tools she has to repair the statue are inadequate: the ladders are small and gluepots are farcical for the work. Here, also, we are told she is using "Lysol," so apparently pieces must not only be put together but disinfection must take place. The god-like image again becomes commonplace (working in conjunction with the colloquial language here), even smelly, and the narrator must also become the traditional female housekeeper. The colossus becomes even larger and more imposing when the narrator describes herself as an ant, crawling and mourning. We hear more detail of how the thirty years have taken their toll. Weeds have infested the statue's brow, his head has become just a skull, and his eyes are not just empty or blank but hopelessly "bald."

Still, the narrator struggles for hope and stability, and she returns again to ancient times. She sees the blue sky, arching over them as "out of the Oresteia," a trilogy of ancient Greek plays. She also compares her statue-father to the Roman Forum, and describes his hair as "acanthine," in the shape of the acanthus leaf that was frequently used as part of the sculptural decor atop ancient Greek columns. Again, then, the narrator makes this colossus part of a great historical tradition—a tradition that revolutionized art, civilization, and government. However, the Greek plays that make up the Oresteia describe horrific jealousy, revenge, and war.

Quickly we are brought back to humble humanity again, as the narrator sits down to her lunch, on a seemingly comfortable "hill of black cypress." The mood cannot be pleasantly simple for long, however, for the narrator describes the hair and bones of the colossus as "littered." The mention of the "bones" here and the previous descriptions of the "skull," "mourning," and "tumuli" (ancient burial mounds) make this not just a ruin but a death.

The narrator describes the enormity of the death, one that could not have occurred just by a "lightning-stroke." Yet amid her despair, there still is some comfort, apparently, for the speaker stays during the nights. We see the intimacy between herself and the colossus when she explains that she is safe squatting in his ear, which can no longer listen but can keep her "out of the wind." Squatting cannot be comfortable for long, we know, yet the ear is described as not only a means of protection from the gusts but as a "cornucopia," the very opposite of ruin and death.

Indeed, by the beginning of the last stanza, the narrator seemingly contentedly counts the rich-hued stars that are "plum-color," the use of the fruit in this description alluding to the cornucopia ear just mentioned. She then admits that while the sun rises, she remains "married" to shadow and, indirectly then, married to her dead father. Also, apparently, if she literally stays in the dark, she does not have to acknowledge others from the live world, whether they be intruders or helpers. Here at the end the narrator says she will not concern herself with listening for their approach—the scrape of a keel on the colossus's stone. The mention of the keel again alludes to the Colossus statue from ancient times, for the statue stood astride a harbor entrance where ships would sail under its legs. In the poem, however, no one can easily sail up to the colossus; instead their approach is an uneasy "scrape" on stones that are "blank." The narrator accepts the colossus and death over others and life. ❀

Critical Views on
"The Colossus"

J. D. MCCLATCHY ON PLATH'S GROWTH

[J. D. McClatchy is a professor of English at Yale University. He is the author of three volumes of poetry and the editor of *Anne Sexton: The Artist and Her Critics*. Here he describes how Plath initially depends on structure in her writing and then moves to experience.]

One way to approach and appreciate the stylistic breakthrough of *Ariel* is to trace some of the recurrences of a single concern—her father, The Father—to its treatment in the book's most famous poem, "Daddy." The plain-prose version is in *The Bell Jar,* whose narrator, Esther Greenwood, "was only purely happy until [she] was nine years old," when her father—who had come "from some manic-depressive hamlet in the black heart of Prussia"—had died. And Esther, on the psychotic verge of suicide, "had a great yearning, lately, to pay [her] father back for all the years of neglect, and start tending his grave." It is only a simple sense of loss, of the horrible distance between the living and dead, that is revealed:

> At the foot of the stone I arranged the rainy armful of azaleas I had picked from a bush at the gateway of the graveyard. Then my legs folded under me, and I sat down in the sopping grass. I couldn't understand why I was crying so hard.
> Then I remembered that I had never cried for my father's death.
> My mother hadn't cried either. She had just smiled and said what a merciful thing it was for him he had died, because if he had lived he would have been crippled and an invalid for life, and he couldn't have stood that, he would rather have died than had that happen.
> I laid my face to the smooth face of the marble and howled my loss into the cold salt rain.

Immediately after this scene, Esther returns from the graveyard, swallows the pills, hides in a cellar hole, and lies down to death: "The silence drew off, baring the pebbles and shells and all the tatty wreckage of my life. Then, at the rim of vision, it gathered itself, and in one sweeping tide, rushed me to sleep." Given the point of view, the emotion here is left distanced and unaccountable, and is told with the restraint that Plath uses throughout the novel to draw out slowly its cumulative effects of disorientation and waste. But the images of stone and sea, sleep and escape, quarry and fear, that structure her account are important. In a memoir written for a 1963 broadcast, "Ocean 1212-W," Plath broods on her relationship with the sea and her earliest self: the miracles of immersion and completion. The birth of her younger brother then defined for her, of her, "the *separateness* of everything. I felt the wall of my skin: I am I. That stone is a stone. My beautiful fusion with the things of this world was over. The tide ebbed, sucked back into itself." And later, at the end: "My father died, we moved inland. Whereon those nine first years of my life sealed themselves off like a ship in a bottle—beautiful, inaccessible, obsolete, a fine, white flying myth."

To watch this myth, these images, resumed in the poems discovers Plath, at first, refining and deepening her metaphor with the precisions of verse. In "The Colossus," the girl clambers in helpless self-absorption over the mammoth ruins of her father:

> Thirty years now I have laboured
> To dredge the silt from your throat.
> I am none the wiser.
>
> Scaling little ladders with gluepots and pails of lysol
> I crawl like an ant in mourning
> Over the weedy acres of your brow
> To mend the immense skull-plates and clear
> The bald, white tumuli of your eyes.
>
> A blue sky out of the Oresteia
> Arches above us.

The figure is right: its immense size symbolizing her incest-awe, its ruined fragments projecting her ambivalent feelings. But the mystery of loss and betrayal, the secretive sexual fantasies, the distortions of knowledge and memory, are left unexplored, dependent solely on the poem's figurative force:

> Nights, I squat in the cornucopia
> Of your left ear, out of the wind,
> Counting the red stars and those of plum-colour.
> The sun rises under the pillar of your tongue.
> My hours are married to shadow.
> No longer do I listen for the scrape of a keel
> On the blank stones of the landing.

It is *The Bell Jar*'s suicidal darkness she curls into here, longing to be reborn into return; it is the same sea that threatens suitors. The same sea that washes through "Full Fathom Five": "Your shelled bed I remember. / Father, this thick air is murderous. / I would breathe water." The same stone in "The Beekeeper's Daughter," a poem addressed to "Father, bridegroom": "My heart under your foot, sister of a stone."

—J. D. McClatchy, "Short Circuits and Folding Mirrors." In *Sylvia Plath*, Harold Bloom, ed. (Philadelphia: Chelsea House Publishers, 1989): pp. 87–89.

TED HUGHES ON PLATH'S POETIC STYLES

[Ted Hughes (1930–1998), poet laureate of England from 1984 until his death, was married to Sylvia Plath. In his introduction to the posthumous publication of Plath's collected works, Hughes gives his perspective on some of the early transitions in Plath's style, while also quoting Plath's own view of her work just around the time of completing "The Colossus."]

By the time of her death, on 11 February 1963, Sylvia Plath had written a large bulk of poetry. To my knowledge, she never scrapped any of her poetic efforts. With one or two exceptions, she brought every piece she worked on to some final form acceptable to her, rejecting at most the odd verse, or a false head or a false tail. Her attitude to her verse was artisan-like: if she couldn't get a table out of the material, she was quite happy to get a chair, or even a toy. The end product for her was not so much a successful poem, as something that had temporarily exhausted her ingenuity. ⟨. . .⟩

⟨N⟩ow on a different kind of inspiration she noted: 'Wrote two poems that pleased me. One a poem to Nicholas' (she expected a son, and titled the poem 'The Manor Garden') 'and one the old father-worship subject' (which she titled 'The Colossus'). 'But different. Weirder. I see a picture, a weather, in these poems. Took "Medallion" out of the early book and made up my mind to start a second book, regardless. The main thing is to get rid of the idea that what I write now is for the old book. That soggy book. So I have three poems for the new, temporarily called *The Colossus and other poems.*'

This decision to start a new book 'regardless', and get rid of all that she'd written up to then, coincided with the first real break-through in her writing, as it is now possible to see. The actual inner process of this quite sudden development is interestingly recorded, in a metaphorical way, in 'Poem for a Birthday', which she was thinking about on 22 October 1959 (cf. note on No. 119). On 4 November she wrote: 'Miraculously I wrote seven poems in my "Poem for a Birthday" sequence, and the two little ones before it, "The Manor Garden" and "The Colossus," I find colorful and amusing. But the manuscript of my [old] book seems dead to me. So far off, so far gone. It has almost no chance of finding a pub-lisher: just sent it out to the seventh. . . . There is nothing for it but to try to publish it in England.' A few days later she noted: 'I wrote a good poem this week on our walk Sunday to the burnt-out spa, a second-book poem. How it consoles me, the idea of a second book with these new poems: "The Manor Garden", "The Colossus", the seven birthday poems and perhaps "Medallion", if I don't stick it in my present book.' ⟨...⟩

The manuscripts on which this collection is based fall roughly into three phases, and each has presented slightly different problems to the editor.

The first phase might be called her juvenilia and the first slight problem here was to decide where it ended. A logical division occurs, conveniently, at the end of 1955, just after the end of her twenty-third year. The 220 or more poems written before this are of interest mainly to specialists. Sylvia Plath had set these pieces (many of them from her early teens) firmly behind her and would certainly never have republished them herself. Nevertheless, quite a few seem worth preserving for the general reader. At their best, they are as distinctive and as finished as anything she wrote later. They can be intensely artificial, but they are always lit with her unique excitement. And that sense of a deep mathematical inevitability in the sound and tex-ture of her lines was well developed quite early. One can see here, too, how exclusively her writing depended on a supercharged system of inner symbols and images, an enclosed cosmic circus. If that could have been projected visually, the substance and patterning of these poems would have made very curious mandalas. As poems, they are always inspired high jinks, but frequently quite a bit more. And even at their weakest they help chart the full acceleration towards her final take-off. ⟨...⟩

The second phase of Sylvia Plath's writing falls between early 1956 and late 1960. Early 1956 presents itself as a watershed, because from later this year come the earliest poems of her first collection, *The Colossus.* ⟨...⟩ Her evolution as a poet went rapidly through successive moults of style, as she realized her true matter and voice. Each fresh phase tended to bring out a group of poems bearing a general family likeness, and is usually associated in my memory with a particular time and place. At each move we made, she seemed to shed a style. ⟨...⟩

The third and final phase of her work, from the editorial point of view, dates from about September 1960. Around that time, she started the habit of dating the final typescript of each poem. ⟨...⟩

I have resisted the temptation to reproduce the drafts of these last poems in variorum completeness. These drafts are arguably an important part of Sylvia Plath's complete works. Some of the hand-written pages are aswarm with startling, beautiful phrases and lines, crowding all over the place, many of them in no way less remarkable than the ones she eventually picked out to make her final poem.

—Ted Hughes, Introduction to *Sylvia Plath: The Collected Poems.*
(New York: Harper & Row, 1981): pp. 13–14, 15–16, 17.

Lynda K. Bundtzen on the Daughter's Opposing Perspectives

[Lynda K. Bundtzen is a professor of English at Williams College. She is the author of numerous articles. In this selection from her book on Plath, she finds confusing the dichotomy of the narrator's perpectives of her father.]

Even in poems that seem to be solely about her personal history, Plath's relationship with her father Otto, we can discern the female "mind of the hive" as a controlling principle of consciousness. The "mind of the hive" is, as we have seen, a "black asininity"—a mindless automatism that fulfills some order imposed from without. Plath creates a sense of secret laws at work in the homely rituals of beekeeping and of a female society with tremendous energies kept under lock and key by these laws.

In an early poem, "The Colossus," and the late "Little Fugue," Plath explores this state of consciousness on a more personal level. Both poems depict a daughter struggling unsuccessfully to recover a dead father, to retrieve his voice and persuade him to speak to her. In both poems, too, Plath evokes a mood of futility. Even if the father could speak, it is implied that he would have nothing to say; and the daughter meanwhile wastes her energies in this obsessive activity directed at giving him life. As in "Daddy," the daughter sacrifices her own vitality to the task of revivifying a dead father.

While both poems are clearly confessional, I would argue that they also illuminate woman's psyche as it is shaped by a patriarchal culture. In "The Colossus," the action takes place under "A blue sky out of the Oresteia," implying that the daughter's personal drama partakes of a tragic and universal lawfulness. In "Little Fugue," the black-and-white order of the world is the father's "Grosse Fuge," and it is duplicated in the daughter's psyche as a little fugue, giving her life a rigid order but no meaning. There is, then, as in the bee poems, a symbiosis between the individual and a larger, oppressive design. Both poems are exemplary expressions, too, of Simone de Beauvoir's description of women's submission to laws they do not understand. ⟨. . .⟩

The daughter in Plath's poems is looking for an oracle, a father who will be the "guarantor of all values" and absolute measure of meaning in her life. At the same time, Plath is critically aware of the fact that her father is nothing but a dead man, a mere mortal. She illuminates the complicity de Beauvoir describes between woman and the man who creates her gods, her laws.

The effect of this double perspective—devoted and critical—in "The Colossus" is confusing. The archaeologist-daughter displays contradictory emotions toward the huge statue she is restoring. At first, she seems totally exasperated with the father and his godlike proportions and pretensions.

> I shall never get you put together entirely,
> Pieced, glued, and properly jointed.
> Mule-bray, pig-grunt and bawdy cackles

Proceed from your great lips.
It's worse than a barnyard.

Perhaps you consider yourself an oracle,
Mouthpiece of the dead, or of some god or other.
Thirty years now I have labored
To dredge the silt from your throat.
I am none the wiser.

In these lines, she appears to be challenging the colossus-father to give her wisdom and comically implies that he has nothing oracular, only animal sounds to utter. She quickly reverses her ironic stance to that of a worshipful suppliant.

I crawl like an ant in mourning
Over the weedy acres of your brow
To mend the immense skull plates and clear
The bald, white tumuli of your eyes.

A blue sky out of the Oresteia
Arches above us. O father, all by yourself
You are pithy and historical as the Roman Forum.

Like the blank mind of God in "Lyonesse," the colossus is a cipher, his eyes expressionlessly "bald" as the clouds in the sky. Even in this state, however, he is a "pithy" god and she is a pygmy living in his colossal body, squatting in his "left ear, out of the wind." While he does not speak, "the sun rises under the pillar of your tongue." It is enough for the daughter to be totally married to her mourning and the task of giving him life.

—Lynda K. Bundtzen, *Plath's Incarnations: Woman and the Creative Process* (Ann Arbor: The University of Michigan Press, 1983): pp. 186–88.

ROBYN MARSACK ON THE POEM'S VIEWS ON OUR UNENDING SEARCHES

[Robyn Marsack is the editor of *Thomas Bewick: Selected Work*. This excerpt from the book she wrote on Plath explores aspects of "The Colossus" and points out that the poem speaks not just of an impossible personal quest but of the lost ideal of Western civilization as well.]

The significance of the statue is clear enough: an enormous figure, catastrophically removed from sight and irrecoverable in its original form. It is close to the small child's view of her wondrous parent— and yet, the dignity of this colossal presence is severely compromised in the poem's first stanza: the giant sounds like a barnyard. I think this is the kind of phrase Ostriker had in mind with regard to 'reducing the verbal glow.'

Furthermore, the tone of the next stanza hovers between the lightly accusing and a wearied impatience: 'Perhaps you consider yourself an oracle . . .'. It is he, not she, who has set himself up as the interpreting voice. But she has colluded, spent all these years clearing his throat. What might this mean in terms of her own use of language?

You might like to look up her story 'Among the Bumblebees' (in *Johnny Panic*), which is very plainly an autobiographical account of the loss of a godlike father; he takes 'Alice' on his back as he swims, and shows her the secrets of bumblebees. The story opens: 'In the beginning there was Alice Denway's father . . .'; the echo of St. John's gospel is deliberate: 'In the beginning was the Word . . . and the Word was God.' The implications for Plath, and for women writers in general, of this linkage of male authority, godlike power and, as it seems, ownership of the language (although, of course, Mary bore the son of God, that is, the Word), is something that feminist critics have illuminatingly explored. Plath tended to link the father-figure with an oracular figure; let me refer you here to the poem 'On the Decline of Oracles', written in 1958 at the same time as 'The Disquieting Muses', both on paintings by de Chirico. The titles suggest a relationship between the disappearance of the male (and his voice) and the ascendancy of the female in her accusing silence. ⟨. . .⟩

The strength of Plath's poem, it seems to me, is that it not only concerns the parent–child relationship, rooted in personal circumstance yet sufficiently unspecific here to allow readers to share the disturbance and pain inherent in the process of apparently unending search, but also that it can be interpreted in a wider sense of a culture's lost direction. Without making grandiose claims for the poem, I think that the sense of irreparable damage done by the two world wars in this century—'more than a lightning-strike'—to an ideal of Western civilization, based on classical foundations, is certainly a presence in the poem. We will return to this matter of Plath's historical imagination.

Working against the 'stony' imagery, the unyielding coldness of the male colossus, are the involuntarily comic noises it emits, and then its fertility and colour by association. 'Cornucopia' gives us an image of the whorled shell of the ear: the horn of plenty in painting spills its fruit, and here we have the surprisingly luscious stars. Is this gesture, sheltering in the remains of something that once sheltered her, a move back into childhood, a terrible admission ('I crawl') of the need for security? We need to judge this in order to know how to read the close of the poem.

'And the long shadows cast by unseen figures—human or of stone it is impossible to tell'—Plath thus described de Chirico. 'My hours are married to shadow': her days are given over to effort that makes no impression, the work of 'an ant in mourning'. It is not possible, I think, to see that as a fruitful effort, although one critic has valiantly maintained that the stone figure, while obstructive, is imperfect, and that the last lines should be read as those of a woman who is no longer content to wait. That seems to go against the grain of the poem: the speaker has given up waiting because she no longer hopes for rescue. There is a sense of exhaustion; the woman herself is perhaps only a 'shadow' of her former self. The landing stones are 'blank' of promise; she will not be setting sail.

—Robyn Marsack, *Sylvia Plath* (Buckingham, Great Britain: Open University Press, 1992): pp. 42–43, 45.

ELISABETH BRONFEN ON THE COLOSSAL WOMB-TOMB

[Elisabeth Bronfen is the author of *The Knotted Subject: Hysteria & Its Discontents* and *Over Her Dead Body: Configurations of Femininity, Death & the Aesthetic*. In this chapter of her book on Plath, she describes the narrator's comfort in escaping the live world for the world of the ruined father. Not only has she left behind other living beings but her meshing with the dead stone father is a precursor to her own death as well.]

In 'The Colossus' Plath returns to her fantasy of re-creating the dead father, only here her idolization of his absent body is presented as a colossal sculpture which she inhabits. A fragmented body which she can never 'put together entirely', the paternal colossus is at the same time an uncanny figure, for from his dismembered mouth are emitted unfathomable yet portentous animal sounds, as though he were reanimated by some unidentified outside force: 'an oracle, | Mouthpiece of the dead, or of some god or other.' Indeed, as Jean-Pierre Vernant argues, the Greek colossus, standing in for the absent corpse, was meant to be a double of the deceased, not a just image but an uncanny figuration bespeaking an ambiguous presence which is also a sign of absence. Rendered in stone, the deceased reveals himself at the same time as he does so by speaking in the language of the beyond. In Plath's version of this Greek practice of substitution, dredging the silt from the colossus' throat so as to facilitate her understanding of the words he speaks from beyond the grave, mending the skull-plates and the white tumuli of his eyes so as to undo the scars of mourning, Plath's persona finds herself fully fusing with this human-shaped ruin. At night she is protected from the wind by squatting in his ear, at dawn she watches the sun rise under his tongue. This shattered figure signifies how her reminiscences allow her only an imperfect configuration of the lost paternal body, with fantasy, however, compensating this fallibility by virtue of exaggerating the individual body parts into inhuman proportions. At the same time, although her incessant mourning produces not just a fragmentary but also an inanimate representation of the father, this stony frame also proves to be a viable shelter from the contingencies of worldy existence. Drawn into its magical sphere, she finds herself turning from the living to the dead. No longer minding signs of other living beings ('the scrape of a keel | On the blank stones of the landing'), she seems to merge with the ruin she cannot mend: 'My hours are married to shadow.' Although, strictly speaking, Plath never gives voice to her dead father, these scenarios, staging her fusion with his dead shape, recall the rhetorical figure of prosopopeia, which, as de Man has so persuasively argued, is inhabited by a latent threat 'namely that by making the death speak, the symmetrical structure of the trope implies, by the same token, that the living are struck dumb, frozen in their own death'. This colossus prefigures not only her own mortality but also her actual entry into the petrified world of the dead, and yet, as in the other father poems, the gesture of self-extinction is inextricably enmeshed with that of poetic creation. The colossal stony figure she enters into as though it were a womb-tomb is a poetic rendition of the psychic representation of the absent father she has incorporated in the course of mourning. As such it is a figure of her own making, so that in these fantasy scenarios revolving around apostrophizing the dead father or responding to his call, refiguration of the dead, self-annihilation, and self-fashioning mutually reverberate.

—Elisabeth Bronfen, *Sylvia Plath* (Plymouth, United Kingdom: Northcote House, 1998): pp. 80–81.

Thematic Analysis of
"The Arrival of the Bee Box"

"The Arrival of the Bee Box" is the second of a five-poem sequence Plath wrote about bees in less than a week in early October 1962. Like most of the other four bee poems and many other poems she wrote that month, it progressed from its first draft to its final version in the space of a single day. Plath planned these to be the last pieces in her *Ariel* book, to end it positively by focusing on survival. Yet while the poems anticipate an optimistic future, they also reflect on Plath's unfinished emotional relationship with her father, Otto, who died when she was a young girl. Otto was a biologist and the author of a book called *Bumblebees and Their Ways*. He was fascinated with the insects, and Sylvia too became a beekeeper and honeygatherer when she was married and living in England.

Issues of power and control, and death and life are immediately in the forefront as "The Arrival of the Bee Box" opens. "I ordered this," the speaker tells us of the box of bees. She has been in charge even before the poem starts, then, and is responsible for the box's arrival, its birth. She takes on the role of parent and must decide what type to be. Yet the box is immediately compared to a coffin, not just any coffin, though, but that of an oddity—a midget or "square baby." The first admittance that this coffin-like box actually contains life does not come until the end of the first stanza, where we are told by the seemingly bothered narrator that there is "such a din in it."

By the second stanza, the box is locked and dangerous. The speaker is distressed that she must "live with it overnight," but at the same time finds it magnetic. There are no windows for her to see "what is in there," and satiate herself. At the same time, there is "no exit," not only for the bees but seemingly for this new keeper of the box.

Still, in the third stanza, the narrator persists in trying to see inside. Putting her eye up to the box's little grid, she is able to make out only darkness. Additionally, though, she says she gets a "swarmy feeling." Now she compares the bees to Africans, "shrunk for export" and "angrily clambering." The speaker is a dictatorial slave master. The bees are only described negatively; the speaker only acts all-powerful. By the fourth stanza, she is frustrated again by the bees' "noise." In truly bigoted fashion, the speaker says they create "unintelligible syllables." As the stanza progresses, the bees are compared to a "Roman mob," which along with the allusion to Africans being exported, has political connotations. Again the narrator is frightened by her prisoners' unified strength, even though, curiously, she holds the key to their prison.

By the fifth stanza the narrator puts her ear to the box, only to hear "furious Latin." Again, then, the bees are angry and labeled as unable to communicate because she cannot understand them. She calls them "a box of maniacs," and realizes that she has the power to send them back and be done with them or even to starve them, for, after all, she pompously announces, "I am the owner."

Yet again, there is a switch in the next stanza, where the narrator wonders not if, but to what degree, the bees are hungry. She even considers letting them go free, but wonders if they would not revolt against her if she did. She imagines that she could turn into a tree such as a laburnum, whose column-like branches would offer some disguise and protection, or whether she could be a cherry tree, whose layers of "petticoats" would create a distance.

Alternatively, in the next stanza, the narrator believes she might be "immediately" safer in "my moon suit and funeral veil," which most probably refers to protective beekeeper apparel. While the description of the attire is odd and again conjures up the coffin from the poem's opening, it is a practical answer, one from a person who truly does, then, know bees. Immediately following is another practical thought, again from a person who knows bees: the bees will not attack her, for she has no honey.

Again, there are twists here, for the line "I am no source of honey" fits our expectation that this malicious speaker could never be a source of anything sweet or good or nourishing. Yet two lines later we are told, "I will be sweet God, I will set them free." We knew that the narrator saw herself as having total control over these bees, so this line is not completely surprising. But what is jolting is her description of herself as "sweet God," although apparently it is fitting if it is true that she will let the bees go. Indeed from the start of the poem, when we were told she must live with the locked bees overnight, we anticipated that these hours would be the only amount of time they would be locked inside. It was only as the poem proceeded that we saw all of the evil of the keyholder, who was so readily toying with different devilish powers.

The poem ends with the only stanza that is just one line: "The box is only temporary." Upon reading this, again we are given the impression that the speaker knew all along that the bees would only be trapped for a short time. There is also a feeling that by freeing the bees, she herself will be free—free of the noise, the responsibility, the nearly endless options—but also free of the evil of being the prison-keeper, the one who originally didn't understand her prisoners. Also, there is the notion that the box, originally seen as a coffin, by being opened is scoffing at death, for when it is opened the inhabitants will be able to be fully alive. This, then, supports the critics' contention that Plath in these later poems, talks not of death as an end but as a chance to be reborn. Similarly, there is the autobiographical view that by opening the box Plath is released of her father. The coffin box is now open, so fretting over his early death is no longer possible. The box that also is alive with bees now has none; their aliveness—and her father's when she was a girl—is no longer confined to her venue; they can be alive in whatever manner they choose without her and she need no longer fear them. ❀

Critical Views on
"The Arrival of the Bee Box"

Rose Kamel on the Bees' Counter-aggression as Political Commentary

[Rose Kamel is a professor in the humanities department at the University of the Sciences in Philadelphia. She is the author of *Aggravating the Conscience: Jewish-American Literary Mothers in the Promised Land*. In this selection, she explains that the bees symbolize helpless, exploited Third World blacks. The poem's narrator is a kind of Pandora, toying with unleashing their violence on the world and recognizing that disaster is imminent for their oppressors as well as possibly for herself.]

Bee life functions as a powerful metaphor. Beekeepers are not only honey gatherers but also social manipulators, and the persona in her *role* as a beekeeper exploits the hive even when she identifies with the workers as females. Indeed, the persona shifts her role often: here she identifies with the queen, there with the workers or the beekeepers. Always the metaphor of bee life expresses the fundamental precariousness of a human psyche that is essentially female. It is not simply that the workers stand for women whose lives are desperate, although on one level the poet means to bring this to our attention. One of the cycle's paradoxes lies in the mercurial shifts of behavior in the bees. Their predictability as animals who behave instinctively becomes questionable when we see how abruptly they change from victims to aggressors and from natural beings to political menaces in their hives. The erratic way the bees respond to what they perceive as dangerous to their collective existence reinforces the way the persona deals with her precarious sense of being. ⟨...⟩

In "Arrival of the Bee Box" and "The Swarm," the victim's counter-aggression takes a political rather than sexual form. In the former the persona-beekeeper contemplates a box of dangerously noisy bees:

> The box is locked, it is dangerous
> I have to live with it overnight
> And I can't keep away from it.

There are no windows, so I can't see what is in there.
There is only a little grid, no exit.

I put my eye to the grid.
It is dark, dark,
With the swarmy feeling of African hands
Minute and shrunk for export,
Black on black, angrily clambering.

How can I let them out?

The bees now resemble exploited blacks in the Third World. Their mood is sustained by a series of link verbs, bound up in a syntax written primarily in the active voice to suggest a much less helpless persona. As a kind of Pandora she toys with the notion of unleashing their violence on the world: "Tomorrow I will be sweet God, I will set them free. / The box is only temporary." Their release, however, would not ensure her safety, for their political instability has a long history:

It is like a Roman mob,
Small, taken one by one, but my God, together!

I lay my ear to furious Latin.
I am not a Caesar.

The "bees'" contemporary restlessness has a historic precedent that portends disaster for Pandora as well as for their political oppressors. Thus she contemplates disguising herself once again—first as a tree, then as a spacewoman:

I wonder if they would forget me
If I just undid the locks and stood back and turned into a tree.
There is the aburnum, its blond colonnades,
And the petticoats of the cherry

They might ignore me immediately
In my moon suit and funeral veil
I am no source of honey
So why should they turn on me?

But she contemplates donning these disguises *after* she has released the bees. The impulse to hide from forces beyond her control like those in "The Bee Meeting" exhibits in "The Arrival of the Bee Box" the "fingers in the ears" gesture of one who has every intention of unleashing violent aggression upon the world.

—Rose Kamel, "'A Self to Recover': Sylvia Plath's Bee Cycle Poems," *Modern Poetry Studies* 4, no. 3 (Winter 1973): pp. 305–6, 310–11.

Mary Lynn Broe on the Power Switch

[Mary Lynn Broe is a member of the English department at Grinnell College. She is the author of *Protean Poetic: The Poetry of Sylvia Plath* (1980), from which this selection is taken. In it she explains the curious twist that occurs in the poem, wherein the bees control their keeper.]

In her six poems about the art of beekeeping, Plath attempts to "recover a self" by exploring the various operations of power within the apiary. The highly organized, self-regulating hive becomes her model for conceptualizing human experience by reexamining power in its many shapes (seller, keeper, worker-drudge), or in its startling absence (queen). The poems suggest that there is a certain truth to psychologist David Holbrook's claim about Plath: "Be(e)ing seems a threat to one who doesn't know how to be." ⟨...⟩

Now in the bee sequence Plath makes her most definitive and ambitious statement about passivity. She suggests that the absence of authoritative power is a form of strength and control, not merely a socially designated trait. Her focus includes only a few relationships and facts: the beekeeper's inept control over the apiary, the deceived workers and virgins, and the royal captive, that bare old queen in hiding whose productive reign over her hive has drawn to a close, but who still remains the focal point both in and outside the colony. While Plath explores the concept of power central to the hive community, her focus is on the ambivalence of the queen. Through this paradoxical symbol of power, she questions the implausible status of heroine in the special category of queen bee, and hence the complexities of a woman artist. For the queen's existence represents a kind of feminocide, a double-edged tribute to uniqueness best described by the workings of apiculture. ⟨...⟩

In contrast to the naiveté of the first two poems, "The Arrival of the Bee Box" is a prosaic study of rational control, of the brag of ownership, of the cheap physical coercion that can reject, kill, or merely unlock: "I ordered this, this clean wood box / Square as a chair and almost too heavy to lift." Assuming the power of the bee-keeper-maestro, the speaker has ordered a box of undeveloped workers and finds herself faced with responsibility for their livelihood. "Tomorrow I will be sweet God, I will set them free," she asserts.

However, she deceives by her "unstable allegorical god-position," for the bulk of the poem reveals the obverse of the power that is authoritarian ownership. The bees control the speaker. As she becomes increasingly fascinated with their vitality and unintelligible noise, she abandons her declared pose of authority. She is lured to imagine various ways to dispose of the vital yet deadly threat:

> I have simply ordered a box of maniacs.
> They can be sent back.
> They can die, I need feed them nothing, I am the owner.

Again, a deathly vitality seems to overshadow any attempt to humorously diminish the contents of the dangerous bee box: the box is bursting with "maniacs," yet they are temporarily contained; they clamber vigorously with a "swarmy feeling," but still suggest decay ("African hands / Minute and shrunk for export"); reduced to a Roman mob chattering Latin, they are frighteningly alien. Whatever assertion of control has been cultivated in the tone, the imagery undercuts it. Her actual power becomes less convincing as her bravado grows. Fear, in fact, prompts her gradual stasis and effacement. She wildly scrambles the boundaries between herself and nature in a total defiance of the maestro's authority:

> I wonder if they would forget me
> If I just undid the locks and stood back and turned into a tree.
> There is the laburnum, its blond colonnades,
> And the petticoats of the cherry.

In the end, her grand resolve to play God is enfeebled by the boisterous liveliness of female drudges. Perhaps it is this sense of the bees' collective vitality that prompts the understated curious promise: "The box is only temporary."

—Mary Lynn Broe, *Protean Poetic: The Poetry of Sylvia Plath* (Columbia: University of Missouri Press, 1980), pp 142, 143, 149–50.

SUSAN R. VAN DYNE ON THE MATERNAL AND PATERNAL TUGS OF WAR

[Susan R. Van Dyne is a professor of English and women's studies at Smith College. She is coeditor of *Women's Place in the Academy: Transforming the Liberal Arts Curriculum*. In this selection from her book on Plath, Van Dyne explains that the bee box represents Plath's own ambivalence about following the lead of her father, who himself was a bee-keeper, and her disturbance at viewing herself exclusively as a biological being.]

In both "The Arrival of the Bee Box" and "Wintering" the powers of creation represented by the bees threaten to become agents of destruction. If the regendered female body could become the corporeal ground of her poetic intelligence, in Rich's terms, the maternal body continued to threaten the poet's extinction. I read the entire bee sequence as Plath's struggle to bring forth an articulate, intelligible self from the potential death box of the hive. ⟨...⟩

To take up beekeeping, and even more to write about it, was deeply resonant for Plath. The bee poems participate in an extended autobiographical narrative that had mythic status for Plath, involving as it did her initiation into starkly polarized gender identities, forbidden desires, and transgressive appropriations of power. They rework the earlier psychodrama she had already reconstructed several times in the 1959 poem "Electra on Azalea Path," in "The Beekeeper's Daughter" from *Colossus*, as well as in a prize-winning undergraduate poem called "Lament," and in her short story from the same period, "Among the Bumblebees." In setting up her own hive in Devon, Plath was self-consciously imitating her father's authority, a mastery she both desires and disdains in "The Beekeeper's Daughter." Keeping bees also served to validate and extend her sense of her own reproductive health. Plath enjoyed the neat parallel that the same woman, Winifred Davies, who taught her beekeeping served as midwife at the birth of Nicholas. Davies also provided significant material help to Plath by securing nannies who would free a few hours a day for her poetry again in October. Written out of the matrix of this layered experience, the bee poems represent not only a revisionary history of her role as daughter, wife, and mother but a simultaneous search for an adequate shape in which to reconstitute herself as both a generative and an authoritative poet. ⟨...⟩

In "The Arrival of the Bee Box" the speaker experiences frightening, uneasy intuitions of a poetic pregnancy. The unknown interior harbors dreadful possibilities: "I would say it was the coffin of a midget / Or a square baby / Were there not such a din in it." Like the shrouded and ominous "awful baby" of "Tulips," the dark, locked box of the body contains archaic mysteries, primitive appetites, and anarchic potential. The beekeeper's doubts about her ability to control what threatens to feed on her mimics a woman's experience of pregnancy which, Kahane suggests, is an inherently Gothic scenario, provoking apprehensions about her bodily integrity as it becomes host to parasitic, alien inhabitants. The grasping, teeming life within would overthrow the conventional, hierarchical authority the speaker has allegedly acquired:

> How can I let them out!
> It is the noise that [terrifies] [appals] [alarms] [dismays]
>   appals me most of all,
> The unintelligible syllables.
> It is like a Roman mob.
> Small, taken one by one, But my god! together!
>
> I [put] lay my ear to furious Latin.
> I am not a Caesar, I am not a Caesar.

Much as she is worried about mothering in this poem, Plath is also wittily experimenting with fathering. She reenacts, with a subversive difference, the role her father played in "The Beekeeper's Daughter." In the earlier poem, the mounting, pulsing sexuality of the female bees threatens to overwhelm the father's capacity to regulate it. The "maestro" in a "frock coat" is an inadequate bridegroom for the queen bee, but still he dominates. In "The Arrival of the Bee Box" the female owner anxiously asserts and retreats from her mastery. When she chooses to claim control, her tone is comically imperious: "They can be sent back, / They can die, I need feed them nothing, I am the owner." Her gestures are self-consciously unmaternal; she can starve or reject these dependent beings rather than teach them speech. This elaborate little dance around the bee box suggests at once Plath's ambivalence about following in her father's footsteps and her antipathy toward defining herself exclusively in terms of her biology.

—Susan R. Van Dyne, *Revising Life: Sylvia Plath's Ariel Poems* (Chapel Hill: University of North Carolina Press, 1993): pp. 104–5, 106–7.

[Malin Walther Pereira is a professor of English at the University of North Carolina at Charlotte. She has published articles on Gwendolyn Brooks, Toni Morrison, and Alice Walker. Here she explains that part of the strength of Toni Morrison's *Tar Baby* is its revision of Plath's bee queen stories. Morrison, she states, provides the truth of the African-American experience, which is distorted and misunderstood by so many revered white American authors.]

In *Playing in the Dark: Whiteness and the Literary Imagination,* Toni Morrison outlines a critical reading practice by which we might study "American Africanism" in canonical (usually white male, sometimes white female) texts. As she defines it, *Playing in the Dark* investigates "the ways in which a non-white, Africanlike (or Africanist) presence or persona was constructed in the United States, and the imaginative uses this fabricated presence served." Morrison's readings of works by Cather, Melville, Twain, Poe, and Hemingway convincingly illustrate how an Africanist presence is used in their works. Ultimately, whatever literary strategies the writers employ, Morrison argues that the "always choked representation of an Africanist presence" in their work is a reflection of the effects of a racialized society on nonblacks; the misreadings, distortions, erasures, and caricatures marking the Africanist presence in nonblack texts say more about the writer's fears, desires, and ambivalences than they state any truth about African Americans. Some critical works have already begun the project Morrison suggests, such as Alan Nadel's *Invisible Criticism: Ralph Ellison and the American Canon,* Dana D. Nelson's *The Word in Black and White: Reading "Race" in American Literature, 1638–1876,* and Eric J. Sundquist's *To Wake the Nations: Race in the Making of American Literature.* Such work needs to expand into exploring the Africanist presence in twentieth-century canonical literature.

The rereadings Morrison calls for can clarify both the racial substructures of texts by significant precursors and the ways Morrison's own fiction responds to the call of her theory. In this essay, I would like to focus on one such response: Morrison's signifying repetition and revision in *Tar Baby* of the bee queen from Sylvia Plath's bee poem sequence in *Ariel,* an intertextual relation which reveals an unacknowledged racial (and racist) dimension in Plath's poetry. Near the end of *Tar Baby*, Morrison describes in some detail the life of the queen of the soldier ants on Isle des Chevaliers. Following directly on the departure of Jadine, the description of the ant queen appears as a commentary on Jadine's quest for self, thereby recalling—in both the image of an insect queen and the theme of female selfhood—Plath's bee sequence. This is of particular significance because many critics have interpreted Plath's bee queen as the emblem for a female self. Rereading through Morrison reveals this self to be a white self, constructed in part by the fear and repression of blackness.

Morrison's repetition and revision of Plath's bee queen in *Tar Baby* uncovers an Africanist presence in Plath's bee poems, a presence unnoticed by Plath critics. Furthermore, fiction, unlike criticism, allows Morrison a space for a corrective revision to such distorted representations of Africanism, a place in which the truth of African American being can be told. ⟨...⟩

In the second poem of the series, "The Arrival of the Bee Box," Plath moves beyond simple color imagery to specifically introduce race. Within the bee box

> It is dark, dark,
> With the swarmy feeling of African hands
> Minute and shrunk for export,
> Black on black, angrily clambering.
>
> How can I let them out?
> It is the noise that appalls me most of all,
> The unintelligible syllables.

Plath's image of the bees as Africans sold to the slave trade draws on the horrors of the middle passage and ultimately appropriates it as a metaphor for female colonization throughout the bee poems. The imagery, furthermore, seems racially stereotypical in its representation of African hands as "swarmy" and the echoes of shrunken heads, both of which connote savagery. Although Plath appropriates slavery as an emblem of her female speaker's colonization within patriarchy, the text fails to critique the speaker's own position as a white colonizer. The speaker, in fact, so fears the bees that she exults in her power over them: "They can be sent back. / They can die, I need feed them nothing, I am the owner." She paints herself a benevolent master in the hope they won't turn on her, promising "Tomorrow I will be sweet God, I will set them free." That the speaker's relationship to the bees is represented through the figures of enslavement and ownership reflects the defining racial discourse informing the poems' epistemology.

The enslaved bees appall the speaker with their communication "noise" that appears to her as "unintelligible syllables." That she cannot perceive their discourse as intelligible recalls Cornel West's observation in *Prophesy Deliverance!* that Western discourse renders African American expression "incomprehensible and unintelligible." West argues that "the idea of white supremacy was constituted as an object of modern discourse in the West," whose underlying logic

> is manifest in the way in which the controlling metaphors, notions, and categories of modern discourse, produce and prohibit, develop and delimit, specific conceptions of truth and knowledge, beauty and character, so that certain ideas are rendered incomprehensible and unintelligible.

Modern Western discourse creates and perpetuates white supremacy in its blindness to alternative ways of knowing. By rendering those alternative conceptions incomprehensible, it effectively delegitimates them and reifies its own discourse. Plath's representation of the bees as unintelligible to the speaker thus disables her from depicting the truth of their be(e)ing. Morrison's parable of the ant queen critiques appropriations like Plath's as limited in their understanding of the racial dimension of Western discourse, and responds by representing the ant queen's point of view as comprehensible and intelligible.

—Malin Walther Pereira, "Be(e)ing and 'Truth': *Tar Baby*'s Signifying on Sylvia Plath's Bee Poems," *Twentieth Century Literature* 42, no. 4 (Winter 1996): pp. 526–27, 529–30.

Thematic Analysis of
"Daddy"

The title of this poem sets its tone from the outset. "Daddy" typically is a name that a child first calls her parent. It is colloquial, lacking the formality and implied respect of "Father." The poem's first line is insistent, frustrated, and full of repetitive sounds, all of which are sustained to the poem's end. It is what one might expect from an angry child or in an incantation—single syllable words repeated with a single-minded purpose. The "Achoo" at the stanza's end also is a word that a child might use instead of the word "sneeze." Critics have commented on the poem's nursery-rhyme-like sound, some believing it marvelously appropriate in light of the childhood reflections, others deeming it a disaster in light of the poem's horrific rage. The poem begins:

> You do not do, you do not do
> Any more, black shoe
> In which I have lived like a foot
> For thirty years, poor and white,
> Barely daring to breathe or Achoo.

At the beginning of the second line there is a switch, which can easily be missed because it is so short and easily rushed over due to the quickness of the poem. But this switch is an early indication of the narrator's own shifting perspectives. "You do not do, you do not do / Any more," the author says. The words "Any more," reveal that this narrator's Daddy was, at some point, acceptable to her.

Now we see that, at the age of thirty (in fact, Plath wrote this just before turning thirty), the narrator is rejecting the life her father made for her, wherein she had no chance to enjoy its riches and was barely able to live. She sees him as black and herself as white; on a basic level they can be no further apart. At the same time, the narrator is saying she no longer wants to be poor, barely able to breathe and, seemingly, white. But if she doesn't want to be white, the alternative, then, is to be less white and more like him. As the poem progresses, such conflicts grow fierce. Some critics have questioned whether the intenseness of the daughter's raw anger at her father actually can coexist with her need for him. Freud and many observers of humanity have answered yes.

Already by the second stanza, the narrator rejects her role as victim and asserts violent revenge. "Daddy, I have had to kill you," she says, and the rather sickeningly controlled, matter-of-fact line sits by itself as a complete sentence on top of the rest of the stanza. Yet the daughter cannot have her way, for, she says, "You died before I had time—." It is almost as if, even with his death, the father has tricked his daughter. Similarly, the reader is tricked here too. For after reading this first sentence, we assume the daughter has killed her father, since she doesn't say "I *wanted* to kill you" or "I *wished* I could kill you" but "I *have had* to kill you" (emphasis added). Only in the next line do we find out that she did not literally kill him. Now we see that "I have had to kill you" was partially a wish and partially means that she has had to kill his remaining presence in her life.

There are numerous autobiographical elements in the poem. Plath's father did die when she was young, from a complication as a result of an operation for a gangrenous toe. The toe is referred to in the poem, as is Nauset, the old name for a town on Cape Cod where her father originally arrived in America from Germany. This section of the poem is one of its few calm spots, both literally and aurally:

> In the waters of beautiful Nauset.
> I used to pray to recover you.
> Ach, du. [translated from German as "Oh, you."]

In attempting to "recover" her father, the speaker says she looked for his history in war-torn Europe but could not find his roots. From this it follows that she herself lacks roots. She speaks not just of never having been able to talk to him, but when she did try, she says, her tongue got stuck in her jaw, "a barb wire snare." This is one of the poem's first Holocaust illusions. The imagery quickly intensifies:

> I thought every German was you.
> And the language obscene
>
> An engine, an engine
> Chuffing me off like a Jew.
> A Jew to Dachau, Auschwitz, Belsen.
> I began to talk like a Jew.
> I think I may well be a Jew.

If the narrator's father is a horrible German, she surmises that she must be the helpless Jewish victim. (This obscures the fact that if her father is German, she too is part German.) Even the German language is obscene and has overwhelming power to the narrator. It takes on the power of an engine. But this is not any engine; it is the engine pulling its train-load of victims to the death camps. As the narration continues, however, even though the daughter says she has always been "scared of *you*," she is less of a victim and more of a chastiser. She starts name-calling, taunting like a girl in a schoolyard who knows she can just run away: "Panzer-man, panzer-man, O You—" ("panzer" originating from the German word meaning "armored"). Then she jeers: "Every woman adores a Fascist, / The boot in the face, the brute / Brute heart of a brute like you." She mocks him as well as sadistic male/female roles overall and their propaganda.

Next she calls her father a devil, and her personal pain returns as she explains that he "Bit my pretty red heart in two." It could be that his evil is what destroyed her heart, or that the pain of his early death is what destroyed it. The poem returns to the autobiographical elements. The narrator says she was young when her father died, and that at twenty she tried to kill herself to "get back, back, back to you." In light of the anger that comes before this point, as one reads this line one almost anticipates that it will say "get back, back, back *at* you," in which case the act of suicide would become twisted revenge. The repetition and the harsh "ack" sound are still violent and desperate, but this time from the daughter who misses her father and needs to return to him; the violence is directed more at the source that has taken him away. The slowness and quiet of the next line reinforces her sad anguish in trying to be near him, even if it meant her own death—"I thought even the bones would do."

After being brought back from death at twenty and prevented from uniting with her father, the narrator is again viciously angry. Out of her need for a paternal figure and as a result of her unresolved issues because her father died when she was so young, she is now connected to a new man who is just like him. She tells her dead father that her husband is "a model of you, / A man in black with a Meinkampf look / And a love of the rack and the screw."

Again she is confronted with a lack of communication, symbolized by the telephone that will not let voices through. The poem is written just after Plath split up with her husband because of another woman. But as much as this man is evil too, she is not a helpless victim here now. While she lived with this "vampire" of a husband for seven years, she has "killed" him, just as she killed/removed her father. She appears triumphant, as she addresses her father, now that he is exorcised from her life: "There's a stake in your fat black heart."

The narrator has removed the horror in her life, and the last line proclaims finality—"Daddy, daddy, you bastard, I'm through." It is as if she is overwhelmingly relieved to be done not only with him but with her husband and with the whole Freudian scenario she was forced to play out. At the same time, the final "I'm through" can mean that she's done in, especially in light of Plath's suicide a few months later. ❀

Critical Views on
"Daddy"

A. Alvarez on Plath's Concern with Loss of
Identity

[A. Alvarez has held several visiting professorships in the
U.S. He has been poetry editor and a regular contributor to
The Observer for many years. He is the author of *The Savage
God: A Study of Suicide,* wherein his prologue offers his personal recollection of Plath. This extract is taken from what
was originally a memorial broadcast on the BBC that was
aired shortly after Plath's death in 1963. In it Alvarez
explains Plath's view of "mass-produced" suffering, as well
as his belief that "Daddy" is a love poem.]

'Lady Lazarus' is a stage further on from 'Fever 103°'; its subject is
the total purification of achieved death. ⟨. . .⟩ But what is remarkable
about the poem is the objectivity with which she handles such personal material. She is not just talking about her own private suffering. Instead, it is the very closeness of her pain which gives it a
general meaning; through it she assumes the suffering of all the
modern victims. Above all, she becomes an imaginary Jew. I think
this is a vitally important element in her work. For two reasons.
First, because anyone whose subject is suffering has a ready-made
modern example of hell on earth in the concentration camps. And
what matters in them is not so much the physical torture—since
sadism is general and perennial—but the way modern, as it were
industrial, techniques can be used to destroy utterly the human
identity. Individual suffering can be heroic provided it leaves the
person who suffers a sense of his own individuality—provided, that
is, there is an illusion of choice remaining to him. But when suffering is mass-produced, men and women become as equal and
identity-less as objects on an assembly line, and nothing remains—
certainly no values, no humanity. This anonymity of pain, which
makes all dignity impossible, was Sylvia Plath's subject. Second, she
seemed convinced, in these last poems, that the root of her suffering
was the death of her father, whom she loved, who abandoned her
and who dragged her after him into death. And her father was pure
German, pure Aryan, pure antisemite.

It all comes together in the most powerful of her last poems, 'Daddy,' about which she wrote the following bleak note:

> The poem is spoken by a girl with an Electra complex. Her father died while she thought he was God. Her case is complicated by the fact that her father was also a Nazi and her mother very possibly part Jewish. In the daughter the two strains marry and paralyze each other—she has to act out the awful little allegory before she is free of it.

'Lady Lazarus' ends with a final, defensive, desperate assertion of omnipotence:

> Out of the ash
> I rise with my red hair
> And I eat men like air.

Not even that defence is left her in 'Daddy'; instead, she goes right down to the deep spring of her sickness and describes it purely. What comes through most powerfully, I think, is the terrible *unforgiveingness* of her verse, the continual sense not so much of violence—although there is a good deal of that—as of violent resentment that this should have been done to *her*. What she does in the poem is, with a weird detachment, to turn the violence against herself so as to show that she can equal her oppressors with her self-inflicted oppression. And this is the strategy of the concentration camps. When suffering is there whatever you do, by inflicting it upon yourself you achieve your identity, you set yourself free.

Yet the tone of the poem, like its psychological mechanism, is not single or simple, and she uses a great deal of skill to keep it complex. Basically, her trick is to tell this horror story in a verse form as insistently jaunty and ritualistic as a nursery rhyme. And this helps her to maintain towards all the protagonists—her father, her husband and herself—a note of hard and sardonic anger, as though she were almost amused that her own suffering should be so extreme, so grotesque. The technical psychoanalytic term for this kind of insistent gaiety to protect you from what, if faced nakedly, would be insufferable, is 'manic defence.' But what, in a neurotic, is a means of avoiding reality can become, for an artist, a source of creative strength, a way of handling the unhandleable, and presenting the situation in all its fullness. When she first read me the poem a few days after she wrote it, she called it a piece of 'light verse.' It obviously isn't, yet equally obviously it also isn't the racking personal confession that a mere description or précis of it might make it sound.

Yet neither is it unchangingly vindictive or angry. The whole poem works on one single, returning note and rhyme, echoing from start to finish:

> You do not do, you do not do ...
> ... I used to pray to recover you.
> Ach, du ...

There is a kind of cooing tenderness in this which complicates the other, more savage note of resentment. It brings in an element of pity, less for herself and her own suffering than for the person who made her suffer. Despite everything, 'Daddy' is a love poem.

—A. Alvarez, "Sylvia Plath," Tri-Quarterly 7 (Fall 1966): pp. 71–72.

Joyce Carol Oates on Plath's Isolation

[Joyce Carol Oates is the Roger S. Berlind Distinguished Professor in the Humanities at Princeton University. A winner of the National Book Award and nominee for the Pulitzer Prize, she has written numerous novels as well as collections of stories, poetry, and plays. Here she explains Plath's tragic belief in the necessity for complete isolation in order for one's uniqueness to survive.]

Sylvia Plath's poems convince us when they are most troubled, most murderous, most unfair—as in "Daddy," where we listen in amazement to a child's voice cursing and re-killing a dead man in a distorted rhythmic version of what would be, in an easier world, a nursery tune. An unforgettable poem, surely. The "parts, bits, cogs, the shining multiples" ("Three Women") constitute hallucinations that involve us because they stir in us memories of our own infantile pasts and do not provoke us into a contemplation of the difficult and less dramatic future of our adulthood. The intensity of "Lesbos" grows out of an adult woman denying her adulthood, her motherhood, lashing out spitefully at all objects—babies or husbands or sick kittens—with a strident, self-mocking energy that is quite different from the Sylvia Plath of the more depressed poems. ⟨...⟩

Sylvia Plath has made beautiful poetry out of the paranoia sometimes expressed by a certain kind of emotionally disturbed person, who imagines that any relationship with anyone will overwhelm him, engulf and destroy his soul. (For a brilliant poem about the savagery of erotic love between lovers who cannot quite achieve adult autonomy or the generosity of granting humanity to each other, see Ted Hughes's "Lovesong," in *Crow*, not inappropriate in this context.)

The dread of being possessed by the Other results in the individual's failure to distinguish between real and illusory enemies. What must be in the human species a talent for discerning legitimate threats to personal survival evidently never developed in Miss Plath—this helps to explain why she could so gracefully fuse the "evil" of her father with the historical outrages of the Nazis, unashamedly declare herself a "Jew" because the memory of her father persecuted her, and in other vivid poems, sense enemies in tulips (oxygen-sucking tulips?—surely they are human!), or sheep (which possess the un-sheep-like power of murdering a human being), or in the true blankness of a mirror which cannot be seen as recording the natural maturation process of a young woman but must be reinterpreted as drawing the woman toward the "terrible fish" of her future self. Sylvia Plath's inability to grade the possibilities of danger is reflected generally in our society, and helps to account for peculiar admissions of helplessness and confusion in adults who should be informing their children: if everything unusual or foreign is an evil, if everything *new* is an evil, then the individual is lost. ⟨. . .⟩

In the summer of 1972 I attended a dramatic reading of Sylvia Plath's "Three Women," given by three actresses as part of the International Poetry Conference in London. The reading was given in a crowded room and, unfortunately, the very professional performance was repeatedly interrupted by a baby's crying from another part of the building. Yet here was—quite accidentally—a powerful and perhaps even poetic counterpoint to Sylvia Plath's moving poem. For there, in the baby's cries from another room, was what Miss Plath had left out: the reason for the maternity ward, the reason for childbirth and suffering and motherhood and poetry itself.

What may come to seem obvious to people in the future—that unique personality does not necessitate isolation, that the "I" of the poet belongs as naturally in the universe as any other aspect of its fluid totality, above all that this "I" exists in a field of living spirit of which it is one aspect—was tragically unknown to Miss Plath, as it has been unknown or denied by most men. Hopefully, a world of totality awaits us, not a played-out world of fragments; but Sylvia Plath acted out a tragically isolated existence, synthesizing for her survivors so many of the sorrows of that dying age—Romanticism in its death throes, the self's ship, *Ariel*, prematurely drowned.

> It is so beautiful, to have no attachments!
> I am solitary as grass. What is it I miss?
> Shall I ever find it, whatever it is?
> ("Three Women")

—Joyce Carol Oates, "The Death Throes of Romanticism: The Poems
of Sylvia Plath," Southern Review 9, no. 3 (July 1973): pp. 517, 520–22.

BRIAN MURDOCH ON THE HISTORICAL USE OF GENOCIDE IMAGERY

[Brian Murdoch has been a member of the English department at the University of Stirling, Scotland. Here he shows writers' treatment of genocide over time, declaring that Plath's use is fitting.]

Sylvia Plath, who wrote her last poems shortly after the appearance of Yevtushenko's "Babi Yar," represents a final stage of development of the Auschwitz imagery. ⟨. . .⟩ Her poetry is without any *engagement*, appropriate or not, and there is no personal justification for her use of the imagery. It is simply the logical aesthetic step into the pure image. The only really surprising feature is the relatively short time in which this step has been accomplished.

It is difficult to separate Sylvia Plath's poetry from her biography—this has become a topos of Plath criticism. It is, however, significant that this kind of biographical positivism has played a part in the evaluations of many of the poems that employ the death-camp imagery, and we are perhaps as justified in looking at Sylvia Plath's own sufferings as a touchstone for her sincerity and lack of cynicism as we are in discussing the background of Abraham Sutzkever as an introduction to his work.

The poem that is most relevant here is the one that has received the bulk of critical attention, "Daddy." Studies of the poem have pointed out, for example, the regularity of its rhythms, nursery rhyme in essence but recalling also the (irregular) beat of the train wheels heard in Celan's "Todesfuge." There are further examples of the same point in other poems from the *Ariel* collection, such as "Getting There," but in "Daddy" Sylvia Plath overtly refers to

> An engine, an engine
> Chuffing me off like a Jew,
> A Jew to Dachau, Auschwitz, Belsen.

The lines merit close consideration: the double meaning of "chuffing me off" (echoing the Shakespearean "shuffling off"?) calls to mind the smoke/air motifs in Sachs and Celan, although the camps have not yet been reached, as it were.

The question of poetic identification is also of concern here. As in Yevtushenko's poem, this identification is tentative, a gradual assumption of the role. The lines cited above continue, "I begin to talk like a Jew." And after the simile, "I think I may well be a Jew." This is then echoed in the next strophe, which ends "I may be a bit of a Jew" and also contains a rare allusion to those other victims of the camps, the Gypsies. ⟨. . .⟩

In some ways, Sylvia Plath comes closer to the horror, even though not directly caught up in it historically, than many of the more involved poets. It is interesting too that she uses the same evocative words out of context: the ash, for example, is prominent at the end of "Lady Lazarus." ⟨. . .⟩

Steiner stresses Sylvia Plath's personal distance from the actual events, and it is through poets like her that the idea of Auschwitz may become a literary (and even lyric) tradition, a metaphor that may today still suggest insensitivity.

There is no reason, however, why the assumption of the "death-rig" should not be honorable, even when there is no memorial intended. Sylvia Plath uses the imagery to underline her own suffering, but a symbol must always carry a concrete meaning of its own. The initial cognitive response provoked by Sylvia Plath's use of Auschwitz imagery serves as a memorial in its own right.

—Brian Murdoch, "Transformations of the Holocaust: Auschwitz in Modern Lyric Poetry," *Comparative Literature Studies* 11, no. 2 (June 1974): pp. 140–41, 146.

ELIZABETH HARDWICK ON PLATH'S REVOLUTIONARY DARING

[Elizabeth Hardwick is a critic, essayist, and founder and advisory editor at *The New York Review of Books*. She edited the letters of William James and wrote a number of books, including *Seduction and Betrayal*. She was married to the poet Robert Lowell for twenty-three years. In this essay, she praises Plath's raw force.]

Is the poem "Daddy" to be accepted as a kind of exorcism, a wild dramatic monologue of abuse screamed at a lost love? ⟨...⟩

Her father died of a long illness, but there is no pity for his lost life. Instead he is not the dead one; he is the murderer. ⟨...⟩

The association of her own pain with that of the Jews in Europe has been named very well by George Steiner, "a subtle larceny." The father did not kill anyone and "the fat black heart" is really her own. How is it possible to grieve for more than twenty years for one as evil and brutal as she asserts her father to have been? On the grounds of psychology every opposite can be made to fall neatly into place—that jagged, oddly shaped piece is truly part of a natural landscape if only you can find the spot where its cutting corners slip into the blue sky. The acrimonious family—yes, any contrary can turn up there, logically as it were. But even strangers, the town, are brought into the punishment of her father and this is somehow the most biting and ungenerous thought of all:

> There's a stake in your fat black heart
> And the villagers never liked you.
> They are dancing and stamping on you.
> They always *knew* it was you.
> Daddy, daddy, you bastard, I'm through.

She insists that she is the victim—poor and white, a Jew, with a pretty red heart. But she is a dangerous and vindictive casualty: "Herr God, Herr Lucifer / Beware / Beware." "Daddy," with its hypnotic rhythms, its shameful harshness, is one of Sylvia Plath's most popular and known works. You cannot read it without shivering. It is done, completed, perfected. All the hatred in our own hearts finds its evil unforgiving music there—the Queen of the Night. ⟨...⟩

Beyond the mesmerizing rhythms and sounds, the flow of brilliant, unforgettable images, the intensity—what does she say to her readers? Is it simple admiration for the daring, for going the whole way? To her fascination with death and pain she brings a sense of combat and brute force new in women writers. She is vulnerable, yes, to father and husband, but that is not the end of it at all. I myself do not think her work comes out of the cold war, the extermination camps, or the anxious doldrums of the Eisenhower years. If anything, she seems to have jumped ahead of her dates and to have more in common with the late 1960s. Her lack of conventional sentiment, her destructive contempt for her family, the failings in her marriage, the drifting, rootless rage, the peculiar homelessness, the fascination with sensation and the drug of death, the determination to try everything, knowing it would not really stop the suffering—no one went as far as she did in this.

> —Elizabeth Hardwick, "On Sylvia Plath." In *Ariel Ascending: Writings About Sylvia Plath*, Paul Alexander, ed. (New York: Harper and Row, 1985): pp. 108, 109, 113.

Jacqueline Rose on the Missing Communication

[Jacqueline Rose has been Professor in English at Queen Mary and Westfield College, University of London. She is the author of *The Case of Peter Pan, or the Impossibility of Children's Fiction*. In this chapter from her book on Plath, she points out the impossibility of communication for the narrator and her father in the poem.]

If this poem is in some sense about the death of the father, a death both willed and premature, it is no less about the death of language.

Returning to the roots of language, it discovers a personal and political history (the one as indistinguishable from the other) which once again fails to enter into words. ⟨. . .⟩

Twice over, the origins of the father, physically and in language, are lost—through the wars which scrape flat German tongue and Polish town, and then through the name of the town itself, which is so common that it fails in its function to identify, fails in fact to name. Compare Claude Lanzmann, the film-maker of *Shoah*, on the Holocaust as 'a crime to forget the name', or Lyotard: 'the destruction of whole worlds of names'. Wars wipe out names, the father cannot be spoken to, and the child cannot talk, except to repeat endlessly, in a destroyed obscene language, the most basic or minimal unit of self-identity in speech: 'ich, ich, ich, ich' (the first draft has 'incestuous' for 'obscene'). The notorious difficulty of the first-person pronoun in relation to identity—its status as shifter, the division or splitting of the subject which it both carries and denies—is merely compounded by its repetition here. ⟨. . .⟩

The effect, of course, if you read it aloud, is not one of assertion but, as with 'ich, ich, ich, ich', of the word sticking in the throat. Pass from that trauma of the 'I' back to the father as a 'bag full of God', and 'Daddy' becomes strikingly resonant of the case of a woman patient described at Hamburg, suspended between two utterances: 'I am God's daughter' and 'I do not know what I am' (she was the daughter of a member of Himmler's SS).

In the poem, the 'I' moves backwards and forwards between German and English, as does the 'you' ('Ach, du'). The dispersal of identity in language follows the lines of a division or confusion between nations and tongues. In fact language in this part of the poem moves in two directions at once. It appears in the form of translation, and as a series of repetitions and overlappings—'Ich', 'Ach', Achoo'—which dissolve the pronoun back into infantile patterns of sound. Note too how the rhyming pattern of the poem sends us back to the first line. 'You do not do, you do not do', and allows us to read it as both English and German: "You du not du', 'You you not you'—'you' as 'not you' because 'you' do not exist inside a space where linguistic address would be possible.

I am not suggesting, however, that we apply to Plath's poem the idea of poetry as *écriture* (women's writing as essentially multiple, the other side of normal discourse, fragmented by the passage of the unconscious and the body into words). Instead the poem seems to be outlining the conditions under which that celebrated loss of the symbolic function takes place. Identity and language lose themselves in the place of the father whose absence gives him unlimited powers. Far from presenting this as a form of liberation—language into pure body and play—Plath's poem lays out the high price, at the level of fantasy, that such a psychic process entails. Irruption of the semiotic (Kristeva's term for that other side of normal language), which immediately transposes itself into an alien, paternal tongue.

—Jacqueline Rose, *The Haunting of Sylvia Plath* (Cambridge: Harvard University Press, 1992): pp. 225, 226–27.

JAHAN RAMAZANI ON PLATH'S REVAMPING OF THE ELEGY

[Jahan Ramazani is a professor of English at the University of Virginia. He is the author of *Yeats and the Poetry of Death: Elegy, Self-Elegy, and the Sublime*. In this piece, he explains how Plath takes off from where her fellow modern elegists left off.]

"Daddy" embodies Plath's ambivalent resistance toward and dependence on the discourse of her father. She combats his fascistic and demonic violence, but her elegy reproduces it in exaggerating his evil and destroying his image. For Plath, patriarchal violence found its ultimate expression in the Nazi death camps, which were the triumph of the victimization from which she suffers. Her father has the same "bright blue" eye as he has in "Little Fugue," and he terrifies her as he does throughout her elegies: "I have always been scared of *you*." But instead of cowering under his massive image, she now fights back. ⟨. . .⟩ Even though Plath's radio comments link "Daddy" to the "Electra complex," his death in this poem is the result less of love than of her need to defend herself from annihilation. Having been victimized by his violence, she now batters him with an equal and opposite aggression. The poem itself makes clear the mirror relation between his and her violence: he "[b]it my pretty red heart in two," and so now she splits open his "fat black heart" with a stake. Much as he seemed to deport her in the Nazi boxcar of his language, she now tries to expel him by her verbal blast. He threatened her by assuming massive proportions, and now she, unlike the tiny "ant in mourning" of "The Colossus," inflates herself by commanding a rhetoric that bullies and bellows; her denunciations, like villagers in a tribal rite, "are dancing and stamping on you." By dying, he abruptly severed the lines of communication between them, and now she, instead of seeking to "get back" to him, tears the telephone "off at the root."

Plath uses the frequently patriarchal discourse of the elegy to banish and kill the patriarch. Although she follows such modern elegists as Yeats, Roethke, Sexton, and Lowell in departing from the eulogistic strain of the elegy, she exceeds their defiance by representing her elegy as an act of murder. ⟨. . .⟩ In addition to the elegiac glorification of the dead, Plath parodies a number of other motifs central to the genre, including compensatory substitution. Having resisted libidinal displacement onto flowers, the sun, or a heavenly soul in her earlier elegies, Plath now fiercely mocks her desire to fashion a surrogate for her dead father. "I made a model of you," she admits, marrying "[a] man in black with a Meinkampf look." Instead of creating yet another substitute, her elegy enacts the destruction of both the original and the copy: "If I've killed one man, I've killed two." Wrecking father and husband-substitute, Plath also demolishes the psychological backbone of the traditional elegy.

—Jahan Ramazani, "'Daddy, I Have Had to Kill You': Plath, Rage, and the Modern Elegy," *PMLA* 108, no. 5 (October 1993): p. 1151.

Elisabeth Bronfen on the Narrator's Confrontation with Her Family History

[Elisabeth Bronfen is the author of *The Knotted Subject: Hysteria & Its Discontents* and *Over Her Dead Body: Configurations of Femininity, Death & the Aesthetic*. This extract from her book on Plath explains the shifts in the "psychic unease" of the narrator of "Daddy."]

With the father now no longer a protective colossus but rather a 'ghastly statue,' a constraining 'black shoe' she has lived in for thirty years, the poetic persona celebrates her belated patricide: 'Daddy, I have had to kill you I You died before I had time.' Yet, even though this new figuration of the dead father is meant to put closure on the process of mourning, in the course of which she had sought to recover him by virtue of imaginatively refashioning him outside the confines of mortal time, the paternal figure continues to function as a phantom, objectifying a gap in her knowledge. As she shifts from describing the ocean as his spectral place of residence to trying to find out the concrete location of his birth, a new gap in knowledge emerges. In this new fantasy scenario, collective and private disaster now come to be enmeshed, given that both his premature death and the two world wars have obliterated any traces of his home town. Not knowing his roots evokes the suspicion that some forbidden knowledge had been at the core of her family even before the traumatic scene of his death occurred, and, in order to mend the gaps in the narrative of her heritage, which she now perceives to be as critical as the father's premature death, she constructs a new family romance. If, in the earlier poems, invoking the lost father allowed her to give a name to her sense that something was awry in her home by blaming his absence, she now locates her psychic unease in the cultural affiliation he represented and had passed on to her. The omnipotent, protective father transforms into his obscene inversion, the terrifyingly brute Nazi stereotype 'panzer-man, O You— I Not God but a swastika' and, as she continues to explore the scene of incest ('Every woman adores a Fascist, I The boot in the face'), she now imagines for herself a Jewish mother, so that, by virtue of an identification with the victim, she can deflect her own guilt about the German ancestry inscribed in her blood. While, in the earlier poems, the father's premature death is the reason she cannot speak to him directly, the cause now is his obscene German language—'a barb wire snare', 'an engine I Chuffing me off like a Jew'—metonymy for a politics of annihilation. At the same time, although Plath's poetic persona transforms her earlier nostalgia for an intact family into a nightmare vision of miscegenation and paternal sadism, with the father cast as a 'devil', a 'man in black with a Meinkampf look', seeking to torture and destroy her, this gothic fantasy is in fact fully consistent with the mythic father portrayed in 'Full Fathom Five', for he, too, is seen as drawing her like a siren to his residence beyond the world of the living.

—Elisabeth Bronfen, *Sylvia Plath* (Plymouth, England: Northcote House, 1998): pp. 82–83.

Thematic Analysis of
"Ariel"

The title of this poem refers to three possible Ariels. First, Ariel is the name of the horse that the narrator of the poem rides, many critics assume, because it also is the name of a horse that Plath herself rode. Second, in the Old Testament, it is the name for the holy city of Jerusalem and means "lion of god." Lastly, in Shakespeare's play *The Tempest* it is the name of a character, a spritely embodiment of poetic imagination who eventually is set free by his master.

While it may be questionable whether the poem's narrator is taking us along on an exhilarating horse ride, what is clear is that the poem is full of incredible movement. It starts in still darkness and then rushes us through shadow that transforms into white, then glitter, and then the blazing red "cauldron of morning." Since morning is the start of day, the poem ends, then, with a beginning and the implication of further movement toward more and more brightness. At the same time, however, the poem ends on what can be seen as a path of suicidal destruction, with the assumption that the narrator will be annihilated by the sun. It is not an accident that "morning" (the last word of the poem) sounds exactly the same as "mourning"—reinforcing the poem's duality and promoting the idea that something must die in order for something new to be born.

Alternatively, some critics have pointed out that it is not death, but the moment of courting death, that is the poem's focus and what fulfills some poets such as Plath. The poem may be about the brink of death, or about sex, or riding a horse, or giving birth to a poem or any other artful work, or any combination of these. What is clear is that it is about the overwhelming ecstasy of escape.

The first line in the poem—"Stasis in darkness."—is the only line that exists by itself, with a period at the end, even though grammatically it actually is not a complete sentence since it lacks a verb. Lacking a verb, it lacks action, which is exactly fitting, for its words are about stillness. The poem, then, starts without movement, and by the second line we are confronted with a word, "substanceless," that is so hard to say that near stillness continues. Yet quickly after this heavy start, however, the pace picks up. Most words in the poem are one or two syllables, most lines are only a few words, and each stanza but one flows into the next.

The second stanza reads:

God's lioness,
How one we grow
Pivot of heels and knees!—The furrow

God's lioness, in any one of the previously mentioned forms, takes the narrator to the place of escape and ecstasy. Quickly, too, the narrator melds with the lioness. The heels and knees of the rider press against her vehicle, give it some direction, and also allow the rider to hold on. Already we are confronted with an exclamation point. But it is in the middle of a line, so we cannot stop for long. The exhilarated riding, sexual allusions, and pure physicality continue as the narrator reaches for "the neck I cannot catch" and gets hauled "through air— / Thighs, hair." Up until this point, though, there is still darkness and also an ominousness. Berries are not just black and sweet but are "Nigger-eye / Berries," full of blood that "cast dark / Hooks" and shadows.

The rider gets pulled through the air by "Something else," into a world that is very different from that of darkness and "Nigger-eye / Berries." The seventh stanza reads:

White
Godiva, I unpeel—
Dead hands, dead stringencies.

"White" on its own line stands in stark contrast to the previous blackness, then, even more so because the narrator has become a white Godiva, showing even more white in her public nakedness. Curious is the choice of the word "unpeel," bringing us back to the previously sweet berries. Also powerful here is the fact that the narrator now exerts some control. She gets to unpeel the deadness rather than just grapple to hold on for the ride. This is the only stanza that stands alone. It is the beginning of the change. The focus is more on light, more on "I." The long "I" sound occurs repeatedly through the rest of the poem, starting with "White" at the beginning of this stanza.

At the start of the next stanza, we read, "And now I / Foam to wheat, a glitter of seas." The concentration on the narrator continues; the unpeeling has produced this new "I" that is light and glimmering, both dry and wet. "The child's cry / Melts in the wall" we are told at the end of the stanza and the beginning of the next. This could be the child that the parent hears while having sex in the next room, whose sound diminishes as the parent becomes more involved with her partner. Or the child could be any possible interruption that might seem to need attention but that disappears after all. The child could also be the young, undeveloped self within the "I" narrator, who now melts into the background as the narrator is transformed.

Near the end of the poem, the narrator becomes "the arrow, / The dew that flies / Suicidal," only to evaporate (harkening back to the child's cry that "melts") as the sun rises. More than one critic has compared the use of the arrow in this poem to the reference to the arrow in Plath's novel *The Bell Jar*. In the novel, the female teenage narrator quotes her boyfriend's traditional mother as saying, "What a man is is an arrow into the future and what a woman is is the place the arrow shoots off from." Later, the young woman (whose life in various ways mimics Plath's) thinks to herself, "The last thing I wanted was infinite security and to be the place an arrow shoots off from. I wanted change and excitement and to shoot off in all directions myself, like the coloured arrows from a Fourth of July rocket."

As the poem progresses, the narrator is "at one with the drive / Into the red / Eye, the cauldron of morning." The escape from the self seems to require coming dangerously close to destruction. The narrator in the poem becomes "at one with the *drive*" (emphasis added) into the red eye, not at one with the actual red eye. The poem ends just on the edge of destruction. Its last lines—"the cauldron of morning"—again point to the mix of destruction and rebirth. Morning traditionally is thought of positively, as a new beginning. Yet here it is a huge, boiling vat, presumably causing destruction as parts of its self are boiled away. At the same time it is an image of cleansing, since boiling traditionally is used as a disinfecting process also. ❀

Critical Views on
"Ariel"

WILLIAM V. DAVIS ON THE ALLUSION TO JERUSALEM

[William V. Davis has been a member of the faculty of the University of Illinois, Chicago Circle. He has written *Robert Bly: The Poet and His Critics,* as well as other works. Here he explains the poem's biblical references and their appropriateness, since Plath is not just describing a horseback ride but ecstasy and revelation.]

"Ariel," the title poem of Sylvia Plath's posthumous volume of the same name, is one of her most highly regarded, most often criticised, and most complicated poems. The ambiguities in the poem begin with its title, which has a threefold meaning. To a reader uninformed by Plath's biography "Ariel" would probably most immediately call to mind the "airy spirit" who in Shakespeare's *The Tempest* is a servant to Prospero and symbolizes Prospero's control of the upper elements of the universe, fire and air. On another biographical or autobiographical level, "Ariel," as we know from reports about the poet's life, was the name of her favorite horse, on whom she weekly went riding. ⟨...⟩

These two allusions, to *The Tempest* and to her horse *"Ariel,"* have often been noticed and pointed out, with the emphasis, from a critical perspective, being placed on the biographical referent. But there is another possible referent in the title of the poem which no one has yet noted, although the poet, apparently, went out of her way to make reference, even obvious reference, to it. I refer to "Ariel" as the symbolic name for Jerusalem. "Ariel" in Hebrew means "lion of God." She begins the second stanza of the poem with the line "God's lioness," which seems to be a direct reference to the Hebrew or Jewish "Ariel."

Plath's obsession with Judaism and the Jewish people is clearly indicated in many of her poems. For instance, in two of her most well-known poems, she makes a point of identifying herself with the Jews and their sufferings, even to the extent that she calls herself (almost certainly erroneously) a Jew. ⟨...⟩

Indeed, some of the imagery which informs the passage concerning "Ariel" in the Book of *Isaiah* (29:1–7) appears to have been drawn on directly by Plath for her imagery in her poem "Ariel." In *Isaiah* 29:5–6 we read,

> And in an instant, suddenly,
> You will be visited by the Lord of hosts
> With thunder and with earthquake and great noise,
> With whirlwind and tempest,
> And the flame of a devouring fire. ⟨. . .⟩

Now, of these three references to "Ariel," the two that seem most fruitful in terms of an analysis of the poem appear to be the autobiographical and the Biblical. ⟨. . .⟩

With respect to the reference to Jerusalem and to "God's lioness," there are several parallels in the body of Plath's poems which make clear her paralleling of a ride on her horse to references to Jerusalem. In an early poem, "The Companionable Ills," from *The Colossus*, she relates imagery of God to horses. ⟨. . .⟩

In another poem, in *Ariel*, Plath aligns some sort of religious ecstasy with horse imagery. This poem, "Years," seems to be closely identified with "Ariel." ⟨. . .⟩

Here, as in "Ariel," the reader is caught up in a mysterious experience which he knows that the *persona* has experienced as a mystery also, but which remains at least partially outside his grasp and beyond his complete knowledge. It is a kind of religious ecstasy and, in that sense, it is a private experience. But Plath wishes to translate the essence of her experience to the reader in as close a way as she can. She wants to communicate the "otherness" of her experience, an "otherness" which she felt in the context of a rather ordinary experience; and, in order to do this, and to remain as honest to the experience as is poetically possible, she resorts to the use of religious imagery to convey the mystery, and, further, she identifies her experience in terms of imagery of horses and horseback riding. She seems to be saying that what she felt, in both of the experiences which stand behind these two poems, was almost like a revelation. Certainly the reader gets the same sort of revelatory experience from "Years" as he does from "Ariel." In both poems the reader senses a similar kind of "stasis in darkness" (and it appears more than an accident that the word "stasis" occurs in both poems) which Plath seems to identify as a religious mystery. In both poems she realizes an emotional and religious "stasis," but both poems, because of the mystery involved, remain somewhat "in darkness." ⟨...⟩

But perhaps the most important structural, as well as thematic, line in the poem is the last line, which is also the final stanza of the poem. This line is important in a three-fold way: first, the "ro" of "cauldron" is inverted to "or" in "morning," thus continuing the duality of the double, and here internal, rhyme that occurs throughout the poem, but at the same time tightening the rhyme even further into the space of a single line; second, the words "eye" and "morning," carrying as they do the overtones of "I" and "mourning," at once incorporate the personal activity (riding a horse) with the communal concern of the Biblical passage (where "Ariel" comes to signify the whole history of the Hebrew race and the suffering, the "mourning" so immediately identified with that history); and, thirdly, the word "cauldron" mixes all of the foregoing elements together into a kind of melting pot of emotion, history and personal involvement. Thus, the poem takes on the richness and complexity we have come to expect from the poet, and, not without reason, stands as the title poem of the book.

—William V. Davis, "Sylvia Plath's 'Ariel,'" *Modern Poetry Studies* 3, no. 4 (April 1972): pp. 176–77, 178, 181, 182–84.

ANTHONY LIBBY ON PLATH'S INTERNALIZATION OF THE APOCALYPSE

[Anthony Libby is an assistant Professor of English at Ohio State University. He has published articles on William Carlos Williams and Robert Bly and is the author of *The Secret Turning of the Earth*. In this extract, he explores Plath's influence on Ted Hughes and vice versa, as well as their perspectives on the mythical mother. Libby also points out that "Ariel" is about one of Plath's repeated themes—the unbearable tension over being both avenger and victim.]

But more often Plath's descent into darkness ends in a rising under the sign of the ascendant Terrible Mother. Her poetry is unusual not so much because of her preoccupation with death, which she shares with countless modern poets, but her references to a mysterious rebirth, ascension not to redemption but to vengeance. ⟨. . .⟩

But the most striking lion image is "God's lioness" in "Ariel." If Hughes's "Cadenza" is an evocation not so much of the personal spirit of Plath as of the underlying terrible Goddess, "Ariel" is an attempt to imagine sexual interaction in terms so transcendent that underlying sexual conflict is resolved in cosmic unity. The poem is more explicitly about sex than has been recognized; the imagery of horseback riding mixes with and then gives way to the imagery of morning lovemaking and orgasm: "I / Foam to wheat, a glitter of seas." "The child's cry / Melts in the wall" can only happen in a bedroom. In such a poem of sexual fulfillment, the devouring Mother cannot appear. But her patterns remain—the female ascent from darkness and stillness into light and motion, the sense of transformation, finally the death that is also rebirth, a fall into cosmic rising. And the ecstasy that ends the poem is "suicidal" not because it involves loss of self into the other—no man actually appears in the poem, and horse and landscape are soon transcended—but because it is a loss of the world; nothing remains but the flow into the rising "cauldron," present sun and fire to come.

So even in a poem which rather beautifully suggests the white magic of Ariel, Hughes's Sycorax, mother of Caliban, looms behind the ascent to triumphant destruction. For Plath's identification with the destructive Mother shapes all her imaginings and shapes her end. For all his adulation of the Goddess, Hughes the male survivor retains—even in the sympathetic *Crow*—an uncontrollable masculine horror at the devouring Mother, an essential suspicion that her violence is excessive, even monstrous. But Plath's instinctive and probably healthy distrust of the Goddess was always undercut by her own femininity, her own motherhood. She was psychologically more vulnerable than Hughes to the Great Mother because she imagined herself as prey, but also because she identified with the vengeful aspect of the archetype. For the vengeance remained inside, and from her death there was no rising. There the identification broke down, with inexorable logic. The female can no more survive destruction of the male principle, external or internal, than men can survive the ongoing destruction of the mythically feminine, whether imagined as mother earth, women, or their own unconscious. As Hughes projected his sense of cosmic violence onto the animal landscape, Plath internalized the apocalypse, became both avenger and victim. Out of the tension between these two roles came much of her most obsessive poetry, poetry often obscure or ambiguous, marked by flashes of genius but also by a certain amount of that oracular confusion that always attends struggle with mysteries. But her poetry is as deep as it is dark and narrow, and it goes to the heart of our time. Her tensions must have been unbearable, but perhaps they were not unique. Without denying the evidence of psychosis we can accept the validity of much of her vision, especially if we agree with R. D. Laing that the schizophrenic experience is largely a heightening of common experience, that the schizophrenic may be more, rather than less, sensitive to the common pressures of existence. Hughes claims the end is already upon us; we have only to look to the world and to ourselves.

—Anthony Libby, "God's Lioness and the Priest of Sycorax: Plath and Hughes," *Contemporary Literature* 15, no. 3 (Summer 1974): pp. 402, 403–5.

D. F. McKay on Plath's Technique for Describing Divine Energy

[D. F. McKay has been a professor of English at the University of Western Ontario. In this extract, he shows how the sounds Plath chooses in "Ariel" so strongly emphasize its subject, the melding of the divine with the everyday.]

The language a poet uses creates order by abstracting from the reality he apprehends. In one sense, then, he must come to terms with an inherited prescriptive syntax. Both ⟨Dylan⟩ Thomas and Plath demonstrate a desire to regain the simultaneity of experience by the strategic manipulation of language: to bring together dancer, the act of dancing and the dance. It is a desire which, related to us on a thematic level, is acted out dramatically by the action of their poems.

Plath's 'Ariel' is, on a superficial level, a poem about the experience of horseback riding at dawn.

        Stasis in darkness.
        Then the substanceless blue
        Pour of tor and distances.

        God's lioness,
        How one we grow,
        Pivot of heels and knees!

Ariel, the horse's name, is also the name given to the city of
Jerusalem by Isaiah (Isaiah 29:7) and means 'God's lion.' Here, deity
is an immanent and coercive animal power, remorselessly pulling the
rider out of her sense of personal identity and into a unity with
itself. From the condition of stasis, produced, perhaps, by riding in
the pre-dawn darkness where the sensation of speed is reduced
because there is no visual gauge, the rider/poet leaps into a condition of absolute kinesis, as though a clutch had suddenly been
released. The line 'Stasis in darkness' aurally enacts the repetitive
churn of the hooves, and 'Pour of tor' blurs sounds just as the
scenery is swept in 'substanceless blue.' The action peels objects
from their substance while it weds the rider to her horse: the
furrow which 'splits and passes' is 'sister to / The brown arc / Of
the neck I cannot catch.'

    Reduced to its psychological content, the poem expresses a con-
ventional death wish, a desire for extinction. But such a characteriza-
tion of the poem ignores the exhilaration due not so much to the
sensation of speed as to the new, purer reality which is momentarily
achieved. The rider/poet becomes agent, act and object, a unity con-
veyed thematically, enacted verbally.

        White
        Godiva, I unpeel—
        Dead hands, dead stringencies.

        And now I
        Foam to wheat, a glitter of seas.
        The child's cry

        Melts in the wall.
        And I
        Am the arrow,

        The dew that flies
        Suicidal, at one with the drive
        Into the red

        Eye, the cauldron of morning.

The linear thrust of the passage is enhanced by the obsessive 'I' sounds, which connect the personal pronoun (I, White/Godiva) of the rider to both action (flies, drive), and its ultimate, obliterating, end (suicidal, red/Eye). Person, act and end are swept into the one driving force by the poet's aural strategy. At the same time, the line lengths are calculated to reinforce the dissolution of the unpeeling 'I,' which is twice left to dangle weakly at the end of the line, to be overwhelmed by the aggressive verbs which follow. The full stress falling upon 'Am' in 'Am the arrow' contributes to the sense of ontological awareness dawning, a new pulse in the insipid copula. The shift from 'I' to the 'Eye' of the rising sun appears to be a metaphysical yoking of disparates, but it is worked out in the passage by syntactical action; the emphasis shifts from the subject 'I' through the action to the object 'Eye,' carrying the reader to this conclusion rather than forcing him into an intellectual leap.

Like most visionary experiences in which the protagonist is invaded by divine power, the flight into the sun constitutes the consummation of being as well as a destruction. Thomas' line 'The sundering ultimate kingdom of genesis' thunder' at the conclusion of 'Ceremony After a Fire Raid' delineates the contradictory constituents of such moments of pure energy. In 'Ariel' we do not pause to distinguish 'destructive' from 'creative' aspects of the 'cauldron of morning': it is a poem about energy itself. But while the energy in 'Ariel' is divine, it is divinity incarnate, springing from a physical event. To the simultaneity of agent, act and object, then, can be added the conjunction of divine and natural worlds, which the title 'Ariel,' God's lion, exemplifies. Like Yeats's 'Leda and the Swan,' 'Ariel' deals with invasion by a power that is both spiritual and brute, but rendered as devastating personal experience rather than myth.

—D. F. McKay, "Aspects of Energy in the Poetry of Dylan Thomas and Sylvia Plath," *The Critical Quarterly* 16, no. 1 (Spring 1974): pp. 54–56.

[Linda Wagner, now Linda Wagner-Martin, is a professor of
English and comparative literature at the University of
North Carolina. She has written two books on Plath as well
as numerous other works on American writers and genres.
She is a co-editor of the encyclopedia *The Oxford Com-
panion to Women's Writing in the United States.* Here she
draws parallels between Shakespeare's Ariel and Plath's
poem, showing how both authors use traditionally negative
symbols in a positive way to reinforce their insistence on the
incredible exuberance of freedom.]

"Ariel," the title poem of the collection that made Plath known to the
reading world so soon after her 1963 suicide, is a similarly
ambiguous poem, rich in its image patterns of movement-stasis,
light-dark, earth-fire. The progression in the poem is from the
simply stated "Stasis in darkness," a negative condition as Plath indi-
cates in the very similarly imaged poem "Years," to the ecstatic trans-
formation-through-motion of the closing. That this is a poem about
motion is clear from the second image, which seems to be a depic-
tion of the faint light of morning ("substanceless blue pour of tor
and distances") yet also stresses the movement of the image—*pour,
distances.* The eye of the reader, like that of the poet, is on what is
coming, and the scene that appears is always couched in imagery
that includes motion words or impressions. Even the furrows of
earth are moving ("splits and passes"). ⟨...⟩

(Because Plath spoke so frequently of her admiration for Shakespeare, and because in another late poem, "The Bee Meeting," she
describes herself as "the magician's girl," it seems a fair assumption
that she did know *The Tempest*; and that, at this period in her life,
separated from her husband and living alone, she might have been
drawn to its fairy-tale emphasis on Miranda's sheltered chastity, and
the final consummation of marriage/peace/brotherhood at the play's
end—even if ironically.)

As Shakespeare describes Ariel, through Prospero's words, "a spirit
too delicate / To act her earthy and abhorred commands," impris-
oned in a pine for a dozen years, until freed from the confinement
by Prospero's "art" (not, significantly, magic or other kind of occult
power). Set in direct and sympathetic contrast to both the hag

Sycorax and Caliban, her son, Ariel is an unrelieved power for freedom and good throughout the play. When he first appears, Act I, Scene ii, he aligns himself with the elements that are presented as positive in Plath's poems:

> All hail, great master! Grave sir, hail! I come
> To answer thy best pleasure, be't to fly,
> To swim, to dive into the fire, to ride
> On the curled clouds. . . .

So succinctly are all the images given, Ariel's speech is a near-abstract for the successive patterns that appear in Plath's poem. And when one relates Ariel's imprisonment within the tree to the "White Godiva, I unpeel" image, even that takes on richer suggestion.

As Ariel continues speaking, we see that the method he has used to effect Prospero's command—to bring the ship to land—is that of taking the shape of fire, St. Elmo's fire ("Now on the beak, Now in the waist, the deck, in every cabin, I flamed amazement. Sometime I'd divide, And burn in many places, on the topmast, The yards and bowsprit, would I flame distinctly, Then meet and join"). The paradox, of course, is that none of the ship's passengers has been harmed, that Ariel's use of fire is a gentle means of attaining what is best for the human beings involved; and that the tone of the play—caught so well in Prospero's farewell charge to Ariel—is that of benevolence and calm. He charges Ariel with securing for the ship at its leave-taking, "calm seas, auspicious gales, And sail so expeditious that shall catch Your royal fleet far off." (The paradox inherent in "auspicious gales" is echoed in Plath's use of fire and driven motion as positive forces within the poem in question.) And to Ariel, as farewell, Prospero adds, with endearment, "My Ariel, chick. That is thy charge. Then to the elements be free, and fare thou well!" The greatest blessing of all, freedom, particularly after a dozen years jailed within a tree. And Plath's vibrant use of the freeflying image at the close of "Ariel" suggests the same benizon, "I / Am the arrow, / / The dew that flies / Suicidal, at one with the drive / Into the red / / Eye, the cauldron of morning." "Then to the elements be free" . . . "at one with the dew." Plath's drive to motion, that sheer impact of energy and force, beyond the "Dead hands, dead stringencies," is the power behind not only "Ariel" but also "Stings," "Lady Lazarus," "Wintering," and "Fever 103°."

—Linda Wagner, "Plath's 'Ariel': 'Auspicious Gales,'" *Concerning Poetry* 10, no. 2 (Fall 1977): pp. 5, 6–7.

[Lynda K. Bundtzen is a professor of English at Williams
College. In this selection from her book on Plath, Bundtzen
asserts that "Ariel" is Plath's "most triumphant assertion of
her poetic powers." Here her poetic transcendence is independent of those issues she frequents in her later work:
vengeance, victimization, and rebirth only through death.]

In "Ariel," the masculine and feminine components of Plath's personality join triumphantly in the figure of a divine androgyne. Here
Plath is capable of sublimating her sexual ambivalence into an essentially hermaphroditic vision of released artistic energy. ⟨. . .⟩

The poem is one of fulfilled desire, of flying thighs and hair and
"Pivot of heels and knees," as in sexual consummation. Her identity
merges with her stallion's Ariel. With her horse, she is a "lioness," but
wears the male lion's mane of a "white Godiva." She is defiantly
female like Godiva, but she assumes the masculine power of her
horse. She is both the female "furrow" of earth, ready to be sown
with male seed, that "splits and passes" and also "the brown arc / Of
the neck I cannot catch." Like Prospero's Ariel, her horse is her muse,
a spirit of fire and air, who can translate desire into action with the
speed of flight, and in flight, she herself metamorphoses into an
arrow of desire.

The evocation of Shakespeare's Ariel is significant, too, for its
implicit statement about woman's creative energy. As Shakespeare's
Ariel is neither male nor female, so the divine activity of the poet is
not a sexual prerogative. It is pure energy, both and neither male nor
female, and belonging to no one. In the moments when the woman
is given over to the apocalyptic fury of her muse, she is also not subject to her feminine roles. Unlike in "Kindness," where Plath feels
compelled by the "child's cry"—"What is so real as the cry of a
child?"—to put her poetry aside and respond, here "The child's cry /
Melts in the wall," forgotten in the flight that takes her to revelation.

The revelation is of a new world created by this rarefied lyric
impulse. As a peal of thunder opens the first seal in God's Book of
Revelation and a white horse with a rider armed in bow and arrows
rides forth, so in "Ariel" Plath begins her creation with the thunder

of a stallion's hooves. The poem is at once about a woman on a run-away stallion, flying dangerously toward the morning's rising sun, and about the divine energy that creates worlds and ends them. The fierceness of "Ariel" is not a surrender to dying, but a sloughing off of the "Dead hands, dead stringencies"—all obstacles—which prevent her incarnation as a divine androgyne. The "suicidal dew," like the incense on the track in "Getting There," is a sacrifice made to the splendor of dawn, to the moment the lyric poet aspires for, when everything has the freshness and illumination of the sun's first light. "Ariel" captures this moment dramatically in the sense of mere duration—"stasis in darkness"—and then the glittering revelation, when everything takes form and perspective from light.

"Ariel" is Plath's most truimphant assertion of her poetic powers, because unlike "Lady Lazarus," "Fever 103°," or "Edge," the transcendence is achieved at no one's expense. It is not a poem directed toward vengeance or turning the tables on a male victimizer, nor does it depict woman's body as a burden to be dragged toward rebirth. She does not simply repossess her body from an old usurpation, but in "Ariel" she is possessed by and in possession of that instant when the Word is incarnated, when the world becomes a vision of energy unfettered by mortal substance, and in Plath's development as a poet, freed from the carnal sting. She is, in this moment, the presiding genius of her own body.

—Lynda K. Bundtzen, *Plath's Incarnations: Woman and the Creative Process* (Ann Arbor: University of Michigan, 1983): pp. 254, 255–56.

SUSAN R. VAN DYNE ON THE INCARNATIONS OF THE SPEAKER IN "ARIEL"

[Susan R. Van Dyne is professor of English and women's studies at Smith College. Here she describes how Plath's drafts of "Ariel" show her movement toward the final version of the poem, where speaker and the animal energy of her horse are nearly one. Van Dyne also explains Plath's choice of the Godiva image. Godiva is an erotic, daring female, yet in this poem, unlike the original legend, no male onlookers exist.]

In "Ariel," Plath is the most reckless in enacting her poetics through the fiery transubstantiation of the female subject. Yet even here creative liberty is expressed through figures that are emphatically corporeal and transgressively sexual. In her drafts Plath progressively obliterates the distance and difference between the speaker and the animal energy of her horse, Ariel, and interpolates a revised legend of Godiva in which the heroic wife performs a rebellious striptease. She also transposes the imagery of burning, first associated with Godiva, to the "red / Eye, the cauldron of morning" in yet another mutation of the poet's volatile form. Each of these changes, I would argue, produces a fusion of poetic identity and the carnal subject, not a rejection of it. The poem originally began by marking more explicitly an initial dichotomy between the raw, unguided material force of the horse and the speaker as controlling, yet desiring subject: "God's lioness also, how one we grow / Crude mover whom I move & burn to love." Compared to the hurtling velocity and unitary drive of the finished poem, the earliest draft reveals a pervasive, unresolved tension between alternative figures for the speaker's transformation in the grip of her muse. ⟨. . .⟩

As she revises, Plath refocuses the poem along a single trajectory, Godiva's daredevil ride at breakneck speed in which horse and rider are merged. The most significant changes occur in the third handwritten draft. The kinship that is claimed at the beginning of the poem ("Sister to the brown arc / Of the neck I cannot catch") is reconfirmed at the close of this draft. The final movement opens with an image in which horse and rider appear to coalesce: "O bright / / beast, I / Am the arrow." The line breaks encourage the reader to interpret this vocative as an appositive, a fluid exchange of identities between radiant carnality and female subjectivity. Plath also reconnects the speaker to flesh in this draft by introducing the figure of Godiva. ⟨. . .⟩

In the legend of Godiva, the importance of her naked ride to relieve the town of her husband's unjust tax is that it is an unseen spectacle. Her body is modestly veiled by her hair, and her chastity is protected by the town's willing refusal, except for peeping Tom, to look. The potency of the icon in the popular imagination, however, is not in its inscription of female purity and its function to validate communal norms of propriety, but precisely in the repressed content of the legend, that is, our fascination with the forbidden image of the unclothed female body as a gesture of female daring and an object of male desire. In her transformation of Godiva, Plath exploits the erotic charge of her self-display and yet refocuses our attention on Godiva as subject rather than spectacle. Plath omits any reference to the male gaze, so prominent in the legend and so essential to "Fever," because she would free her speaker even more unequivocally from this dependence. In the single stanza Plath retains in the final poem, Godiva is defiantly antisocial, her desire an unconstrained liberty of self-definition: "White / Godiva, I unpeel— / Dead hands, dead stringencies." She is unashamed of her guilty pleasure in the exhilarating ride that eludes even maternal obligations and ignores the child's cry that "melts in the wall."

—Susan R. Van Dyne, *Revising Life: Sylvia Plath's Ariel Poems* (Chapel Hill: University of North Carolina, 1993): pp. 119–20, 121–22.

Thematic Analysis of
"Lady Lazarus"

There are some elements in "Lady Lazarus" that are so autobio-
graphically based that they must be acknowledged from the start.
The poem is about attempting suicide; it speaks of close calls with
death at the ages of ten, twenty, and thirty, and Plath did nearly die
from an accident at age ten, tried to kill herself at twenty, and pur-
posefully ran her car off the road at thirty. The poem was written in
the frenzy of October 1962, when Plath was separated from her husband, Ted Hughes, and wrote nearly a poem a day just prior to her
thirtieth birthday at the end of the month. "Lady Lazarus" is just one
of numerous poems that has a voice radically distinct from that in
Plath's previous work, which was more controlled, impersonal, and
traditional.

The poem's title, its final line, and much of what is in between,
focus on annihilation, rebirth, and female power. Its title refers to
the biblical story in which Christ brought Lazarus back from the
dead. However, in this poem, it is a woman who comes back from
the dead—on her own—without the help of a male/God figure. Not
only has she brought herself back from the dead, but she has done it
three times (a number that has some significance in the Bible, also).

Curiously, the poem starts with the disarmingly colloquial comment about her power to bring herself back from the dead: "I have
done it again." The ability to bring someone back to life—what is
usually construed as a divine power—has become humanized and
almost too easy. But the narrator is not a human who has stolen
divine power but one who just happens to have it. The feeling is
reinforced by the narrator's modest "I *manage* it," as well as her
description of herself as a "*sort of* walking miracle" (emphasis
added).

Quickly, there is a shift in tone. Now the narrator is not just a
victim of suicide who has made it back. Instead, it looks like she is
not the only one responsible for this, her third death, for her skin is
compared to "a Nazi lampshade" and her face a "featureless, fine /
Jew linen." She speaks now to "O my enemy" and asks "Do I terrify?"
The narrator is far from just happy to be alive, then, but has another
quest—revenge on her murderers. With this third rebirth has come

courage. Later in the poem, allusions to the Holocaust will recur and intensify. Some critics, however, have found them highly inappropriate for the poem, a desperate grasp for a horrific image. Others see the imagery as both valuable for a poem about much more than one woman's suicidal view and also as applicable in a modern brutal world.

Again, we are struck with a strong shift in tone in the middle of the ninth stanza.

> Now it seems we are at a circus:
> The peanut-crunching crowd
> Shoves in to see
>
> Them unwrap me hand and foot—-
> The big strip tease.
> Gentlemen, ladies
>
> These are my hands
> My knees.
> I may be skin and bone,
>
> Nevertheless, I am the same, identical woman.

The narrator, now, is on display, a side-show act who is also her own promoter and announcer. She asks for attention from the audience that shoves in for the spectacle, wanting to look at something they know they shouldn't, a person stripped of herself. Theirs is a cruel symbiotic relationship. At the same time, again there are references to Christ. He had been wrapped before being placed in his grave. His hands and feet were left scarred from the nails driven into them by his persecutors to hold him on the cross. Upon his resurrection, his doubtful disciple said he would have to feel and see Christ's scars in order to believe him alive.

By the next line, the narrator is no longer the circus barker but addresses her reader directly. She explains that her first death was an accident, but that the second time she "meant / To last it out and not come back at all." She doesn't talk of the third death here, but comments on death overall: "Dying / Is an art, like everything else. / I do it exceptionally well." The ironic twist here is that dying is not really the art; what attracts the peanut crunchers is the fact that the narrator is reborn. Coming back to life, not dying, is the art. In fact, dying can be seen as what the narrator does exceptionally poorly, since it never lasts. Of course, without it the rebirth could never take place.

Just as the narrator tells us that when she is reborn she is the "same, identical woman," now many lines later she reiterates that she comes back

> To the same place, the same face, the same brute
> Amused shout:
>
> "A miracle!"
> That knocks me out.

There is now apparently some comfort in knowing she will come back as herself. And despite the fact that she still is herself, her onlookers are always amazed. The exclamation here of "'A miracle!'" is especially vibrant in comparison to the line at the poem's beginning where the narrator describes herself as "A sort of walking miracle." The narrator, then, has gotten something out of this crowd, it is not just naked embarrassment but exhilaraton. But we are told that "There is a charge / For the eyeing of my scars, there is a charge / For the hearing of my heart— / It really goes." The crowd must pay for their look, just as the narrator must also pay a price to keep these parts of her self alive.

As the poem comes closer to its end, the Nazi analogy returns. The narrator provokes her persecutors with: "So, so, Herr Doktor. / So, Herr Enemy." ("Herr" is "Mister" in German.) The use of "Doktor" alludes to the horrendous experiments that the Nazis performed on their prisoners. But then the narrator becomes the victim, "The pure gold baby / That melts to a shriek. / I turn and burn." Still, she is the one whose sarcasm cannot be subdued. "Do not think I underestimate your great concern," she says with bravado, since she knows she is reborn, no matter how horrifically she has been killed. But we cannot escape the deathly ovens so quickly. The enemy pokes in the ash at the narrator, where little is left, just a list, the first of which is "A cake of soap," what the inhuman Nazis would make from the remains of their victims.

Yet this narrator is not to be victimized so readily after this, her death "Number Three." Now her persecutors are not evil Nazis; Nazis were not enough of a challenge. Now her enemy is actually God, as well as Lucifer. God and Lucifer, in fact, may be one here. After this third death, the narrator comes back consumed with vengeance and now makes her victims as insignificant as they had wanted to make her. Their destruction helps sustain her and it is so very easy.

Herr God, Herr Lucifer
Beware
Beware.

Out of the ash
I rise with my red hair
And I eat men like air. ❀

Critical Views on
"Lady Lazarus"

ROBERT BAGG ON PLATH'S REFUSAL TO ACCEPT THE
SELF'S LIMITATIONS

[Robert Bagg had been part of the English Department at
the University of Massachusetts. A widely published poet,
his first volume of poetry, *Madonna of the Cello,* was nomi-
nated for the National Book Award. In this selection, he
comments on Plath's freeing of the self through imagined
self-annihilation.]

In "Lady Lazarus" she makes a "self" in a poem which is more alive,
more menacing than any poem I can recall. She becomes so menacing by taking literally the cliché that a poet is immortal in his
works. After death she knows she will be found nowhere else. What
Sylvia does is to accept utterly this convention and speak in the
poem with the peremptory malice of an avenging voice even from
the dead. She mocks the reader's curiosity about her death and then
she counter-attacks the male sensibility which must read her. ⟨...⟩

The reader finds himself harangued in this death-camp of a
poem. If we are curious, if we want to touch her "ashes" or listen to
her heartbeat (really going she assures us as she writes) we will
have to pay; we pay for the "large charge" we vicariously get from
watching this strange bitter woman. The price we must pay is to
sense that our macabre awe at the way she presents herself—as an
"imaginary Jew" cremated to bones and ash—marks our complicity in the masculine version of human life she finds so
degrading. Our shock that she so hates the system of life imagined
by the male that she feels it as a Jew would an extermination
camp—surely one of the most outrageous metaphors ever—confirms
for her our uncritical commitment to it. She makes us see that she
is a live woman writing the poem who will die into its images, the
blood, bone and ash, to nothingness, and then rise as a fierce consciousness accosting and taunting us in the poem's speech. We are
Christ to her Lady Lazarus; we are the air she breathes, because our
minds give her her new life; she eats us as a flame eats air—her
imagination inflames our conscience. A remarkable *trompe l'âme,* a

manipulation of the reader's soul to enter the brutal room of her mind, as collaborator in her death.

All the poets I've considered ⟨Yeats, Eliot, and Lowell⟩ have searched for some firm ground, some situation of leverage from which the self might cope, at least in the intense arena of a poem, with the forces that would cripple and obliterate it. In the case of Sylvia's three predecessors, their varying solutions have had this in common: they acknowledge, in one form or another, that their conception of the self, governed by religious or metaphysical allegiances, always incurred a diminution, a partial defeat for the self fighting to preserve its autonomous happiness. Sylvia, however, who finds the world more insidious and intolerable than any of the others, is not bound by any metaphysical belief in the self's limitations. Instead of resisting the self's antagonists she derives a tremendous thrill from throwing her imagination into the act of self-obliteration. The energy, the creative inflaming of particular images, with which she endows the process is immense. Since her imagination is committed to annihilation of the self trapped in life, the self present in her willed imagined destruction survives, not only free and intact, but ecstatic. Hence, "Dying / is an art," not something the self must await in frozen acquiescence.

—Robert Bagg, "The Rise of Lady Lazarus," *Mosaic* 2, no. 4 (Summer 1969): pp. 34, 35–36.

IRVING HOWE ON PLATH'S WEAKNESS

[Irving Howe (1920–1993) was Distinguished Professor of English at Hunter College. He wrote many works of literary criticism, including books on Faulkner, Hardy, and Sherwood Anderson. He also edited numerous literary volumes, as well as works on politics and Judaism. In this selection from one of his books, he writes that Plath's violent, hysteric tone in her confessional poetry is an attempt to make up for its other weaknesses. Still, he points out, her talent is notable.]

At times Sylvia Plath also wrote confessional poetry, as in the much-praised "Lady Lazarus," a poem about her recurrent suicide attempts. Its opening lines, like almost all her opening lines, come at one like a driven hammer:

> I have done it again.
> One year in every ten
> I manage it—
>
> A sort of walking miracle, my skin
> Bright as a Nazi lampshade,
> My right foot
>
> A paperweight,
> My face a featureless, fine
> Jew linen.

The tone is jeringly tough, but at least partly directed against herself. There is a strain of self-irony ("a sort of walking miracle") such a poetry of this kind can never have enough of. Still, one must be infatuated with the Plath legend to ignore the poet's need for enlarging the magnitude of her act through illegitimate comparisons with the Holocaust. ⟨. . .⟩

Sylvia Plath's most notable gift as a writer—a gift for the single, isolate image—comes through later in the poem when, recalling an earlier suicide attempt, she writes that they had to "pick the worms off me like sticky pearls." But then, after patching together some fragments of recollection, she collapses into an archness about her suicide attempts that is shocking in a way she could not have intended:

> I do it so it feels like hell.
> I do it so it feels real.
> I guess you could say I've a call.
>
> It's easy enough to do it in a cell,
> It's easy enough to do it and stay put.

As if uneasy about the tone of such lines, she then drives toward what I can only see as a willed hysteric tone, the forcing of language to make up for an inability to develop the matter. The result is sentimental violence:

> A cake of soap,
> A wedding ring,
> A gold filling.

. . . . . .

Out of the ash
I rise with my red hair
And I eat men like air.

In the end, the several remarkable lines in this poem serve only to intensify its badness, for in their isolation, without the support of a rational structure, they leave the author with no possibility of development other than violent wrenchings in tone. And this is a kind of badness that seems a constant temptation in confessional poetry, the temptation to reveal all with one eye nervously measuring the effect of revelation. ⟨. . .⟩

That her story is intensely moving, that her talent was notable, that her final breakthrough rouses admiration—of course! Yet in none of the essays devoted to praising Sylvia Plath have I found a coherent statement as to the nature, let alone the value, of her vision. Perhaps it is assumed that to enter the state of mind in which she found herself at the end of her life is its own ground for high valuation; but what will her admirers say to those who reply that precisely this assumption is what needs to be questioned?

After the noise abates and judgment returns, Sylvia Plath will be regarded as an interesting minor poet whose personal story was poignant. A few of her poems will find a place in anthologies—and when you consider the common fate of talent, that, after all, will not be a small acknowledgment.

—Irving Howe, *The Critical Point of Literature and Culture* (New York: Horizon Press, 1973). Reprinted in *Sylvia Plath*, Harold Bloom, ed. (New York: Chelsea House, 1989): pp. 9–10, 15.

JON ROSENBLATT ON THE SOUNDS OF THE POEM

[Jon Rosenblatt has been an assistant professor of English at Rhode Island College. Here he shows examples of Plath's aestheticism in her late work, focusing on her word choice and her use of rhyme, form, and rhetoric.]

"Lady Lazarus" defines the central aesthetic principles of Plath's late poetry. First, the poem derives its dominant effects from the colloquial language. From the conversational opening ("I have done it again") to the clipped warnings of the ending ("Beware / Beware"),

"Lady Lazarus" appears as the monologue of a woman speaking spontaneously out of her pain and psychic disintegration. The Latinate terms ("annihilate," "filaments," "opus," "valuable") are introduced as sudden contrasts to the essentially simple language of the speaker. The obsessive repetition of key words and phrases gives enormous power to the plain style used throughout. As she speaks, Lady Lazarus seems to gather up her energies for an assault on her enemies, and the staccato repetitions of phrases build up the intensity of feelings:

> I do it so it feels like hell.
> I do it so it feels real.
> I guess you could say I've a call.
>
> It's easy enough to do it in a cell.
> It's easy enough to do it and stay put. ⟨...⟩

The colloquial language of the poem relates to its second major aspect: its aural quality. "Lady Lazarus" is meant to be read aloud. To heighten the aural effect, the speaker's voice modulates across varying levels of rhetorical intensity. At one moment she reports on her suicide attempt with no observable emotion:

> I am only thirty.
> And like the cat I have nine times to die.
> This is Number Three.

The next moment she becomes a barker at a striptease show:

> Gentlemen, ladies,
> These are my hands.

Then she may break into a kind of incantatory chant that sweeps reality in front of it, as at the very end of the poem. The deliberate rhetoric of the poem marks it as a set-piece, a dramatic tour de force, that must be heard to be truly appreciated. Certainly it answers Plath's desire to create an aural medium for her poetry.

Third, "Lady Lazarus" transforms a traditional stanzaic pattern to obtain its rhetorical and aural effects. One of the striking aspects of Plath's late poetry is its simultaneous dependence on and abandonment of traditional forms. The three-line stanza of "Lady Lazarus" and such poems as "Ariel," "Fever 103°," "Mary's Song," and "Nick and the Candlestick" refer us inevitably to the terza rima of the

Italian tradition and to the terza rima experiments of Plath's earlier work. But the poems employ this stanza only as a general framework for a variable-beat line and variable rhyming patterns. The first stanza of the poem has two beats in its first line, three in its second, and two in its third; but the second has a five-three-two pattern. The iambic measure is dominant throughout, though Plath often overloads a line with stressed syllables or reduces a line to a single stress. The rhymes are mainly off-rhymes ("again," "ten"; "fine," "linen"; "stir," "there"). Many of the pure rhymes are used to accentuate a bizarre conjunction of meaning, as in the lines addressed to the doctor: "I turn and burn. / Do not think I underestimate your great concern."

Finally, "Lady Lazarus," like "Daddy" and "Fever 103°," incorporates historical material into the initiatory and imagistic patterns. This element of Plath's method has generated much misunderstanding, including the charge that her use of references to Nazism and to Jewishness is inauthentic. Yet these allusions to historical events form part of the speaker's fragmented identity and allow Plath to portray a kind of eternal victim.

—Jon Rosenblatt, *Sylvia Plath: The Poetry of Initiation* (Chapel Hill: University of North Carolina Press, 1979): pp. 40, 41–42.

FRED MORAMARCO ON THE LITERAL DESTRUCTIVENESS OF PLATH'S LATER STYLE

[Fred Moramarco is a professor of English and Comparative Literature at San Diego State University. He has published numerous articles on modern and contemporary American poetry, fiction, and drama. Here he agrees with the perspective that Plath's earlier poetry—with its more distanced style—actually aided in keeping her alive.]

The poems in *The Colossus* are generally regarded as carefully crafted technical exercises, their concerns far removed from the self-destructive, morbid obsessions which emerge in *Ariel* and *Winter Trees.* ⟨. . .⟩ Yet looking beyond the technical expertise of the *Colossus* poems, one sees the same suicidal fixations, the same willingness to look death straight in the eyes, the same impressions of the natural, inanimate world as indifferent to human concerns, immense in its power and seductive in its tranquility. The difference between Plath's earlier and later work is largely a difference in technique, but that difference, as Hugh Kenner has wryly observed, may be a very large difference indeed: "[A]s long as she worked in the manner of *The Colossus* she kept safely alive. One prefers one's poets kept alive." Critical of Ted Hughes's notion that his wife's late habit of "top speed" writing freed her imagination from the restraints of her earlier, more conventional writing habits, Kenner writes: "What had, in Ted Hughes' phrase, 'worked mainly against her' was a set of habits that, if I read aright, had kept her producing and alive."

The habits that kept Plath producing and alive are indeed set aside in the later poems in which the seductress Suicide sheds her garments one by one to tantalize us with the simplicity and purity of the naked self. The readers of these poems become the "peanut-munching crowd" of "Lady Lazarus," shoving in to see

> The big strip tease.
> Gentlemen, ladies,
> These are my hands,
> My knees.
> I may be skin and bone,
> Nevertheless, I am the same, identical woman.

The poet of *Ariel* is indeed the same identical woman who wrote *The Colossus*, and there is not a rupture between these two books, but rather, as Marjorie Perloff has noticed, a shedding of masks, a movement closer to the austerity and purity of her single subject: "her own anguish and consequent longing for death."

From the perspective of most literary criticism, however, it is tempting—even essential—to ignore the fact that the writer of these harrowing self-revelatory lyrics took her own life. Judith Kroll, for example, in her stimulating study of Plath's work argues for the necessity to approach the work objectively as literature and tell us that "the fact . . . that she killed herself is irrelevant to the consideration of the meaning of her work; as literature the poems would mean what they do even if she had not attempted suicide." ⟨. . .⟩ According to Kroll:

> Virtually all of the apparent "death wishes" in her late poems have the ambiguity of a simultaneous wish for rebirth, which can only be achieved through some kind of "death." It is not that life is unacceptable, "that life, even when disciplined is simply not worth it" (as Robert Lowell says in his foreword to *Ariel*), but that life lived on the wrong terms, a life lived by the false self, is not life but an intolerable death-in-life which can be overcome only by dying to that life. The late poems are really exploratory attempts to release the true self and to establish an authentic existence.

Such a reading of the poetry may be appropriate in terms of positivistic "human potential" psychology—the "false self" must die so that the "true self" can live—but it ignores the fact that the purveyor of those sentiments annihilated both aspects of her divided life. If the true self is "released" only to destroy itself one has to question the validity of the search.

Plath's most famous lines from "Lady Lazarus" as well as the title and overall impressions of that poem clearly take on additional resonance when read with the knowledge of her actual suicide on February 11, 1963. The poem deals with a lifelong flirtation with suicide, and like the Lazarus of the title, its persona miraculously survives each brush with death. The lines, "Dying / Is an art, like everything else / I do it exceptionally well," are often cited as the center of Plath's obsession, but Plath's actual suicide mocks their efficacy. Dying, of course, is not an art, though writing well about dying is, and it is the latter, not the former, that Plath did exceptionally well. Her actual suicide attempts were botched and gruesome, and even her final completion of the act was possibly, according to A. Alvarez, a botched attempt to call attention to herself.

—Fred Moramarco, "'Burned-up intensity': The Suicidal Poetry of Sylvia Plath," *Mosaic* 15, no. 1 (Winter 1982): pp. 146–48.

[Lynda K. Bundtzen is a professor of English at Williams
College. She has written numerous articles. In this selection
from her book, she explains that "Lady Lazarus" is an allegory about the female author's struggle for independence.]

These multiple, contradictory relationships between Lady Lazarus
and both her audience and her creator are resolved in the last four
stanzas of the poem. Still another Lady Lazarus emerges from the
Nazi ovens, very different from the personalities we have seen so
far. ⟨. . .⟩

In the final invocation to Herr God, Herr Lucifer, there is no self-
mockery. She is in deadly earnest. The warning "Beware" sounds as
though a dangerous circus animal has escaped and refuses to per-
form anymore. The lioness turns on trainer and audience alike,
baring her claws instead of her wounds, and revealing her untamed
powers for the first time. She gives everyone a bigger "charge" than
they wanted or expected.

With this shift in tone, there is a reversal on all levels of the action.
Lady Lazarus is resurrected twice, first as the "opus," the "valuable"
of Herr Doktor, the clumsy artist of paperweights and lampshades.
Again he melts her down to the accumulated trash of her life—"A
cake of soap, / A wedding ring, / A gold filling"—and pokes and
stirs, thinking he might create something from the ashes. But "there
is nothing there." He misses the flamelike exhalation from the oven
and the incarnation of Lady Lazarus as a body of fire, a man-eating
phoenix woman. The Jewess turns on her Nazi oppressor. The
stripteaser who pleases men transforms herself into a man-eater.
The scapegoat becomes a predator. And most important, the cre-
ator-creature relationship that supersedes all others in this poem is
inverted. The creature takes over the task of resurrection and is her
own miracle. It is as if Lazarus were to say, "I'd rather do it myself."

From this perspective, "Lady Lazarus" is an allegory about the
woman artist's struggle for autonomy. The female creature of a male
artist-god is asserting independent creative powers. Next to Lady
Lazarus's miraculous rise at the end, the male god's art is an inept
engineering feat. Where at the beginning of the poem the Lady

merely manifests his potency—indeed, prostituting her imagination by playing the role of female exhibitionist—by the end of the poem she is a creator in her own right.

Given the shifting and complex set of relationships that Plath sets up in "Lady Lazarus," it seems a waste to dwell overlong on the poem's confessional aspects, to worry about whether this or that stanza refers to some incident in Plath's life, or to belabor the fact that Herr God may be a representation of her father or her husband. Whatever his origins in the circumstances of Plath's life, in this poem he is the usurper of Lady Lazarus's artistic powers, and he is defeated on those grounds.

It is important to note as well that Lady Lazarus is not simply an escape artist. She directly confronts and challenges Herr God at the end of the poem with her own self-resurrection, and this new self is surely less monstrous than Herr God's swaddled cadaver. As a poem about overcoming the woman writer's anxiety of authorship, "Lady Lazarus" provides a new reading of the monster-woman. She is neither mad nor "ugly and hairy," but a phoenix, a flame of released bodily energy. The insanity was her complicity in Herr God's sleazy sideshow, not in the choice of self-incarnation. Just as the male author allays his anxieties by calling their source bad names—witch, bitch, fiend, monster—so Plath allays her anxieties by identifying the father-god with Nazi brutality, calling him Herr Doktor, Herr Enemy, Herr Lucifer, or, in "Daddy," "a man in black with a Meinkampf look."

—Lynda K. Bundtzen, *Plath's Incarnations: Woman and the Creative Process* (Ann Arbor: University of Michigan Press, 1983): pp. 32–34.

ALICIA SUSKIN OSTRIKER ON PLATH'S SOLUTIONS FOR DETACHMENT

[Alicia Suskin Ostriker is a professor of English at Rutgers University. She has written *Vision and Verse in William Blake*, as well as numerous works of poetry. In this selection from her book on women's poetry, she describes Plath's answers for escaping one's body and one's world: poetic manipulation and/or death.]

⟨In Plath's poetry the⟩ drama of social and political life plays out, on a nightmarishly large scale, the victimization of the body.

Plath imagines the possibility of detachment from body and world in two ways. The first of these is the distancing of experience through poetic manipulation; the second is death. In some of the late poems, these solutions coalesce.

The modern masters had taught the superiority of art to the absurdity of life, and Plath in the 1950s was a good student. Her early verse employs tight formal structures, bookish diction, an armory of allusions to sanctioned works of art and literature, and a consistently ironic impersonality of tone, which has everything to do with controlling experience, little to do with dwelling in it. The looser, less traditional forms of her late work intensify rather than relax our sense of the poet's control. She manipulates rhyme and off-rhyme, regular and irregular meter, with the casualness of a juggler tossing knives, and her mature mastery of colloquial idiom illustrates her contempt for the vulgar and cruel social relations which generate such idiom. She becomes a mocker of the vernacular, using language against itself. ⟨...⟩

As Plath's artistic control increased, so did her vision of possible release, into a state of purification and perfection equivalent to the perfection of art. ⟨...⟩ And in *Ariel*, the poet "unpeels" herself from her body in poem after poem, lets her body "flake" away, annihilates the "trash" of flesh which disgusts her because it would make her kin to the ogling peanut-crunching crowd. She transforms herself from gross matter to "a pure acetylene virgin" rising toward heaven or to dew evaporating in the sunrise—but transcendence always means death. When self-inflicted, it spells triumph. And if she fears and scorns death's perfection as well as life's imperfection ("Perfection is terrible, it cannot have children"; "This is what it is to be complete. It is horrible"), self-annihilation is nevertheless the ultimately artistic, ultimately ironic response to humiliation.

Had Plath lived, she might have discovered another exit from the locked compartment; possibly through motherhood, about which she wrote her only poems of unambiguous sensual pleasure. As it is, she imagined one further form of transcendence. The veiled and jadelike woman in "Purdah," who says of her bridegroom "I am his," proceeds to envision herself the tigress who will kill him. The daughter in "Daddy" who lives passively and fearfully "like a foot," adores "the boot in the face," and lets her "pretty red heart" be bitten in two, finally accomplishes her ritual murder of the father she loves and hates. "Lady Lazarus" reduces Lucifer, God, the killer of Jews, and the poet's doctor to a single brutal exploitative figure. Given the poem's title, this figure is also the one who in the Gospels raises Lazarus, speaks of laying up treasures in heaven, and is himself resurrected after death. 〈. . .〉

In the Plath scheme, then, if transcendence is a solution to the problem of the body, it merely means joining the killers instead of the killed. It is not this vision which de Beauvoir anticipates when she asks women to "attack the world." But when the physical self is made an object, trash, subject to harm and worthy of destruction, its most ardent impossible dream may be to destroy its maker.

—Alicia Suskin Ostriker, *Stealing the Language: The Emergence of Women's Poetry in America* (Boston: Beacon Press, 1986): pp. 101, 102–3.

Works by Sylvia Plath

The Colossus and Other Poems. 1960.

The Bell Jar. (published under the pseudonym Victoria Lucas) 1963.

Ariel. 1965.

The Bell Jar. (published in Plath's name) 1966.

Crossing the Water and *Winter Trees.* 1971.

Letters Home: Correspondence 1950–1963. 1975.

The Bed Book. 1976.

Johnny Panic and the Bible of Dreams: Short Stories, Prose, and Diary Excerpts. 1977.

The Collected Poems. 1981.

The Journals of Sylvia Plath. 1982.

The It-Doesn't-Matter Suit. 1996.

Works About
Sylvia Plath

Aird, Eileen. *Sylvia Plath.* New York: Barnes and Noble, 1973.

Alexander, Paul, ed. *Ariel Ascending: Writings About Sylvia Plath.* New York: Harper and Row, 1985.

Axelrod, Steven Gould. "The Drama of Creativity in Sylvia Plath's Early Poems." *Pacific Coast Philology* 32 (1997): pp. 76–86.

Axelrod, Steven Gould. "The Mirror and the Shadow: Plath's Poetics of Self-Doubt." *Contemporary Literature* 26 (Fall 1985): pp. 286–301.

Bawer, Bruce. "Sylvia Plath and the Poetry of Confession." *New Criterion* 9 (1991): pp. 18–27.

Besdine, M. "Jocasta Complex, Mothering and Women Geniuses." *Psychoanalytic Review* 58 (1973): pp. 51–74.

Boyers, Robert. "Sylvia Plath: The Trepanned Veteran." *Centennial Review* 13 (1969): pp. 138–53.

Brink, Andrew. "Sylvia Plath and the Art of Redemption." *Alphabet* 15 (1968): pp. 48–69.

Broe, Mary Lynn. "'Oh Dad, Poor Dad': Sylvia Plath's Comic Exorcism." *Notes on Contemporary Literature* 9 (1979): pp. 2–4.

Burnham, Richard E. "Sylvia Plath's 'Lady Lazarus.'" *Contemporary Poetry* 1 (1973): pp. 42–46.

Cam, Heather. "'Daddy': Sylvia Plath's Debt to Anne Sexton." *American Literature* 59 (October 1987): pp. 429–32.

Coulthard, A. R. "A Biblical Allusion in Plath's 'Lady Lazarus.'" *Notes on Contemporary Literature* 21 (November 1991): p. 3.

Cunningham, Stuart. "Bibliography: Sylvia Plath." *Hecate* 1 (July 1975): pp. 95–112.

Dale, Peter. "'O Honey Bees Come Build.'" *Agenda* 4 (Summer 1966): pp. 49–55.

Davis, Robin Reed. "The Honey Machine: Imagery Patterns in *Ariel.*" *New Laurel Review* 1 (Spring 1972): pp. 23–31.

Easthope, Anthony. "Reading the Poetry of Sylvia Plath." *English* 43 (Autumn 1994): pp. 223–35.

Ferrier, Carole. "The Beekeeper and the Queen Bee." *Refractory Girl* (Spring 1973): pp. 31–36.

Gilbert, Sandra M. "Teaching Plath's 'Daddy' to Speak to Undergraduates." *ADE Bulletin* 76 (Winter 1983): pp. 38–42.

Graham, Vicki. "Reconstructed Vase: Sylvia Plath and the New Critical Aesthetics." *Texas Review* 15 (Spring–Summer 1994): pp. 44–65.

Hampl, Patricia. "The Smile of Accomplishment: Sylvia Plath's Ambition." *Iowa Review* 25 (Winter 1995): pp. 1–29.

Herman, Judith B. "Plath's 'Daddy' and the Myth of Tereus and Philomela." *Notes on Contemporary Literature* 7 (1977): pp. 9–10.

Holbrook, David. "Out of the Ash: Different Views of the 'Death Camp'—Sylvia Plath, Al Alvarez, and Viktor Frankl." *The Human World* 5 (November 1971): pp. 22–39.

Hoyle, James F. "Sylvia Plath: A Poetry of Suicidal Mania." *Literature and Psychology* 18 (1968): pp. 187–203.

Howes, Barbara. "A Note on *Ariel.*" *Massachusetts Review* 8 (Winter 1967): pp. 225–26.

Kenner, Hugh. "Ariel—Pop Sincerity." *Triumph* 1 (September 1966): pp. 33–34.

Kurtzman, Mary. "Plath's 'Ariel' and Tarot." *Centennial Review* 32 (Summer 1988): pp. 286–95.

Lane, Gary, and Maria Stevens. *Sylvia Plath: A Bibliography.* Metuchen, N.J.: Scarecrow Press, 1978.

Lindberg-Seyersted, Brita. "Dream Elements in Sylvia Plath's Bee Cycle Poems." *American Studies in Scandinavia* 22 (1990): pp. 15–24.

Lord, Mae Masket and Carole Stone. "Fathers and Daughters: A Study of Three Poems." *Contemporary Psychoanalysis* 9 (August 1973): pp. 526–39.

Malcolm, Janet. *The Silent Woman: Sylvia Plath and Ted Hughes.* New York: Afred Knopf, 1994.

Martin, Wendy. "God's Lioness—Sylvia Plath, Her Prose and Poetry." *Women's Studies* 1 (1973): pp. 191–98.

McCann, Janet. "Sylvia Plath's Bee Poems." *South and West* 14 (1978): pp. 28–36.

Meissner, William. "The Rise of the Angel: Life Through Death in the Poetry of Sylvia Plath." *Massachusetts Studies in English* 3 (Fall 1971): pp. 34–39.

Mollinger, Robert N. "A Symbolic Complex: Images of Death and Daddy in the Poetry of Sylvia Plath." *Descant* 19 (Winter 1975): pp. 44–52.

Morris, Christopher. "Order and Chaos in Plath's 'The Colossus.'" *Concerning Poetry* 15 (Fall 1982): pp. 33–42.

Nance, Guinevara, and Judith P. Jones, "Doing Away with Daddy: Exorcism and Sympathetic Magic in Plath's Poetry." *Concerning Poetry* 11 (1978): pp. 75–81.

Newman, Charles, ed. *The Art of Sylvia Plath.* Bloomington: Indiana University Press, 1971.

Perloff, Marjorie. "The Two Ariels: The (Re)Making of the Sylvia Plath Canon." *American Poetry Review* 13 (November–December 1984): pp. 10–18.

Phelps, H. C. "Sylvia Plath's 'Polack Friend': The Ambiguous Geography, History, and Ethnic Hierarchies of 'Daddy.'" *Notes on Contemporary Literature* 26 (January 1996): pp. 7–8.

Platizky, R. "Plath's Daddy." *Explicator* 55 (Winter 1997): pp. 105–7.

Sarot, Ellin. "To Be 'God's Lioness' and Live: On Sylvia Plath." *Centennial Review* 23 (Spring 1979): pp. 105–28.

Schwartz, Murray M., and Christropher Bollas. "The Absence at the Center: Sylvia Plath and Suicide." *Criticism* 18 (1976): pp. 147–72.

Skei, Hans H. "Sylvia Plath's 'Lady Lazarus': An Interpretation." *Edda* 4 (1981): pp. 233–44.

Smith, Nigel. "Sylvia Plath's 'Daddy.'" *English Review* 1 (September 1990): pp. 16–17.

Srivasta, K. G. "Plath's 'Daddy.'" *Explicator* 50 (Winter 1992): pp. 126–28.

Taylor, Andrew. "Sylvia Plath's Mirror and Beehive." *Meanjin* 33 (September 1974): pp. 256–65.

Wood, David. "Art as Transcendence in Sylvia Plath's *Ariel.*" *Kyushu American Literature* 24 (May 1982): pp. 25–34.

Index of
Themes and Ideas

"AMONG THE BUMBLEBEES," 36

"ARIEL," 58–73; Ariel in, 58, 61–63, 64, 67, 68–69, 70, 72; arrow in, 60; artistic energy in, 68–71; as autobiographical, 58, 61, 62; biblical references in, 58, 61–63, 66, 70; critical views on, 61–73; death/destruction in, 58, 60, 64, 66–67; and divine energy, 65–67, 71; ecstasy in, 58, 59, 64, 68; escape in, 58, 59; freedom in, 68–69, 73; Godiva image in, 59, 67, 70, 72–73; horseback riding in, 58, 62, 64, 65–66, 70–71, 72; "I" in, 59–60, 63, 66–67; incarnation of speaker in, 71–73; internalization of apocalypse in, 63–65; lioness in, 58, 59, 61, 62, 64, 66, 67, 70, 72; morning/mourning in, 60, 63, 68; movement in, 58–59, 65–66, 68, 69; sexuality in, 58, 59, 60, 64, 70, 72–73; and Shakespeare, 61, 68–69, 70; thematic analysis of, 58–60; three-line stanza of, 82

ARIEL, 13, 18, 29, 38, 49, 83, 84, 88

"ARRIVAL OF THE BEE BOX, THE," 23, 29–40; as autobiographical, 31, 36; bees as Africans in, 29–30, 32–34, 38–40; bees controlling keeper in, 34–35; coffin image in, 29, 30, 31; control in, 29, 30, 34–35; critical views on, 32–40; death/life in, 29, 31; father in, 29, 31, 36–37; freeing bees in, 30–31, 33; maternal/paternal tugs of war in, 36–37; thematic analysis of, 29–31; worker bees as women in, 32

BED BOOK, THE, 14

"BEEKEEPER'S DAUGHTER, THE," 20, 36

"BEE MEETING, THE," 33, 68

BELL JAR, THE, 12, 13, 18–19, 60

COLLECTED POEMS, THE, 14

COLOSSUS AND OTHER POEMS, THE, 12, 62, 82–83

"COLOSSUS, THE," 15–31; and ancient times, 15, 16, 17; colossus/father in, 15–17, 19–20, 23–24, 26–28, 55; colossus womb-tomb in, 26–28; critical views on, 18–31; death in, 16–17, 26–28; disinfection in, 15–16; figurative force of, 19; and impossible personal quest, 24–26; language in, 16; and lost ideal of Western civilization, 24–26; thematic analysis of, 15–17; and title, 15

"COMPANIONABLE ILLS, THE," 62

CROSSING THE WATER, 13

"DADDY," 41–57; as autobiographical, 42, 43–44; critical views on, 18, 45–57; and elegy, 54–55; family history in, 55–57; father in, 18, 23, 41–44, 46, 51, 52–56, 89; Holocaust in, 42–43, 46–47, 49–50, 51–52, 53, 54–55, 56, 83; husband in, 43, 44, 46, 52; impossibility of communication in, 52–54; and isolation, 47; as love poem, 46–47; nursery-rhyme-like sound of, 41, 50; raw force in, 51–52; suicide in, 43, 44; thematic analysis of, 41–44; transcendence in, 89

DOUBLE EXPOSURE, 13

"EDGE," 71

"ELECTRA ON AZALEA PATH," 36

"FEVER 103°," 45, 69, 71, 73

"FULL FATHOM FIVE," 19–20

"GETTING THERE," 50, 71

IT-DOESN'T MATTER SUIT, THE, 14

JOHNNY PANIC AND THE BIBLE OF DREAMS: SHORT STORIES, PROSE, AND DIARY EXCERPTS, 14

JOURNALS OF SYLVIA PLATH, THE, 14

"KINDNESS," 70

"LADY LAZARUS," 74–89; annihilation in, 74, 78–79; aural quality of, 82; as autobiographical, 74; biblical references in, 74, 75, 78, 89; colloquial language in, 81–82; as confessional poetry, 80–81, 87; critical views on, 46, 71, 78–89; and detachment, 87–89; father in, 45; and female authorship, 86–87; female power in, 74; Holocaust in, 45, 50, 74, 75, 76, 78, 80, 83, 86, 87; motion in, 69; omnipotence in, 46; rebirth in, 74–77, 87; sounds of, 81–83; suicide/death in, 45, 74, 75–76, 78–79, 80, 84–85; thematic analysis of, 74–77; three-line stanza of, 82–83; weaknesses in, 80–81

"LAMENT," 36

"LESBOS," 47

LETTERS HOME: CORRESPONDENCE 1950–1963, 14

"LITTLE FUGUE," 23, 54

"LYONESSE," 24

"MANOR GARDEN, THE," 20, 21

"MEDALLION," 20, 21

"OCEAN 1212-W," 19

PLATH, SYLVIA: biography of, 11–14; destructiveness of later style of, 83–85; growth of, 18–22; and Hughes, 63–65; isolation of, 47–49; poetic eminence of, 9–10; weakness of, 80–81

"POEM FOR A BIRTHDAY," 21

"PURDAH," 89

"STINGS," 69

"SWARM, THE," 32

THREE WOMEN, 13, 14, 48

"WINTERING," 36, 69

WINTER TREES, 13–14, 83

"YEARS," 61–62